Light
Back-
packing

Light Back-packing

DONALD CHRISTIAN

Winchester Press
Tulsa, Oklahoma

LIBRARY OF CONGRESS CATALOGING IN PUBLICATION DATA
Christian, Donald.
   Light backpacking.

   Includes index.
   1. Backpacking.   2. Backpacking—Equipment and
supplies.   I. Title
GV199.6.C45   796.5'1   81-378
ISBN 0-87691-338-9   AACR1

Published by Winchester Press
1421 South Sheridan
P.O. Box 1260
Tulsa, Oklahoma 74101

Book design by Quentin Fiore
Printed in the United States of America

1 2 3 4 5   85 84 83 82 81

Acknowledgments

I would like to thank these people for all their help in this endeavor:

Pam MacKesey and the Cornell Plantations, Emil Ghinger, Atley Nesbitt and Nippenose of Ithaca, Bob Wesley, Pete Contuzzi, Alex Lange, Ed Finegan, and Sue Bissell.

Special thanks to Dan Kahn-Fogel and Judy Abrams without whom this book would not have been possible.

Contents

Introduction

I have tried to write this book as clearly and simply as possible. It is a compilation of information on methods of camping and backpacking, information that I have gathered, for the most part, from personal experience. I included what I hope is a manageable number of options for ways to go about the various activities.

The book is not written for veteran backpackers — a little experience is better than ten books. It is aimed at the novice, ideally to be read before he spends a lot of money unnecessarily and has a miserable three days in the woods, wet, cold, and blistered. I have purposely omitted a discussion of the winter season; first, because I believe that winter backpacking is an entire subject in itself, what with cross-country skis, snowshoes, and all; and second, because the winter is not the time for a first venture out into the bush.

Along with the acquired knowledge necessary for entering the outdoors, I've tried to incorporate some information about the ingenuity, resourcefulness, and reasoning powers of the North American Indian, whom I consider to be the greatest of all outdoorsmen and -women.

Why go backpacking? The urge to "get back to nature" came to North America along with the first Europeans:

> In his *History of the Five Indian Nations* (1727) Cadwallader Colden was at a loss to account for why so many white prisoners of the wars of 1699 and 1700 could not be persuaded to go back to the clearings; try as he would, he was unable to think of a single comparable instance of an Indian choosing to remain with the English.... Why was it "thousands of Europeans are Indians and we have no example of even one of those aborigines having from choice become European?" Could there really be "something superior in Indian society?"... In his *Danger of Apostacy* (1679), Increase Mather had come perilously close to letting the cat out of

the bag: "People are ready to run wild into the woods again and be as heathenish as ever, if you do not prevent it."
(*Memoirs of a Captivity Among the Indians of North America*, John Dunn Hunter, edited by Richard Drinnon, p. xv)

Go ahead, be heathenish. What better way could there be to spend your free time?

What advantages has the man in the brown stone front over the man in the tent? Only these: a pale face instead of the brown skin which is natural to his species; a coated tongue, no appetite, and no digestion, instead of the keen zest for food and splendid digestive vigor of the tent dweller; and aching head and confused mind and depressed spirits, instead of the vim and snap and energy, mental and physical, and the freedom from pain and pessimism of out-of-door dwellers; early consumption or apoplexy or paresis or cancer of the stomach or arteriosclerosis – the dry rot of the body which stealthily weakens the props and crumbles the foundations of the citadel of life.
(*Learning from the Indians*, Wharton James, p. 66)

When I am backpacking, I feel my best. I've never gotten sick while backpacking, though I have walked in wind, rain, and snow; waded through glacial streams; exhausted myself climbing mountain trails; and taken enough food for only three days and stayed out seven. Your physical condition cannot help but improve from the combination of fresh air and exercise. Your endurance will increase tremendously each day you are out hiking. The endurance of the Indians who lived out year-round was truly astonishing:

It is no uncommon thing for an Oraibi or Mashonganavi to run from his home to Moenkapi, a distance of forty miles, over the hot blazing sands of a real American Sahara, there hoe his cornfield, and return to his home, within twenty-four hours. I once photographed, the morning after his return, an old man who had made this eighty-mile run, and he showed not the slightest trace of fatigue.

For a dollar, I have several times engaged a young man to take a message from Oraibi to Keam's Canyon, a distance of seventy-two miles, and he has run on foot the whole distance, delivered his message, and brought me an answer within thirty-six hours.

One Oraibi, Ku-wa-wen-ti-wa, ran from Oraibi to Moenkapi, thence to Walpi, and back to Oraibi, a distance of over ninety miles in one day.

I doubt not that most of my readers suppose that these experiences are rare and unusual, and come after special training. Not at all! They are regular occurrences, made without any thought that the white man was either watching or recording. When asked for the facts, the Indians gave them as simply and as unconcernedly as we might tell of a friend met or a dinner eaten. And it is not with one tribe alone. I have found the same endurance with Yumas, Pimas, Apaches, Navahos, Havasupais, Wallapais, Chemahuevis, Utes, Paiutes, and Mohaves. Indeed, on the trackless wastes of the Colorado desert, the Mohaves and Yumas perhaps show a greater endurance than any people I have ever seen!
(*Learning From the Indians*, Wharton James, pp. 79–80)

Besides improving your physical condition, going into the wilderness will give you the chance to slow down from the rapid pace of living that now exists in most of our country. You will have the time to appreciate the dawn and the stars, watch some animal life, and really relax.

I hope this book helps to make your first few backpacking trips more enjoyable and rewarding.

Donny

Light Back-packing

1. Choosing and Caring for Equipment

A WORD ON GEARING UP

The most trying experience you will probably have on your first backpacking trip will come before you set foot on a trail: the visit to your local equipment store. Because backpacking has become so popular in recent years, the variety of equipment and choice of brands is truly bewildering. Many people make the mistake of "heavy overkill" before they have ever been backpacking, and end up paying a lot of money for equipment that would be necessary only for the most rigorous arctic expedition. Remember, all you really need to spend a few days comfortably outdoors are a blanket and a knife. This short description was found in the saga of a poor guy who had no choice of equipment to take on his first hike:

> It is perhaps worthy of notice, that although I had been little accustomed to exposure, had never been subjected to trails and hardships such as I was now compelled to undergo; yet no injurious effect on my health ensued from wading creeks, falling into the water, lying out in the open air, in all kinds of weather, nor from any other inconvenience, which I encountered in the course of this long and painful march, the first I had ever made on foot.
> (*Held Captive by Indians: Selected Narratives, 1642–1836*, edited by Richard Vander Beets, p. 272)

To begin with, you can probably borrow or rent a tent, sleeping bag, and backpack, giving yourself a chance to decide which items you would eventually like to own. It has been my experience that the fewer gadgets and pieces of equipment you have to carry, worry about, and rely on, the better. Over the course of a few outings, needed equipment will become obvious.

Start simply, and after you have taken a few trips, gradually add more equipment to your collection. Don't burden yourself with a lot of unnecessary weight and complication when you start, or you will find your first camping trip frustrating and exhausting. I have seen backpackers on their first trip lugging eighty pounds of equipment, including all the latest "wilderness contraptions," and twenty or so pounds of the newest camera equipment. They were truly miserable. So was one fellow's poor dog, which had to carry an overloaded pack as well. Remember, when you are hiking, every extra pound will make a difference, so keep the pieces of equipment to a minimum.

There are many considerations for selecting equipment, and there is a lot of equipment—all kinds of clothing, shelter, and tools of different types for different climates, seasons, uses, people, and places. Depending on where and when you go, *you* have to make the decisions about whether or not, and if so, what kind and how much. I acquire clothing, equipment, and tools very, very slowly, and only after carefully considering whether or not I really need them.

If you are trying to save money, there are good kits on the market for sewing your own backpack, tent, poncho, and other gear. You will need access to a sewing machine, but the instructions in the kits are basic enough so that you don't need to be an experienced sewer. I have made a backpack, a vest, and a two-man tent and have found there are other advantages to these kits besides their prices. I can reinforce areas that I know will take a lot of stress, and I also know how the item fits together and thus how to repair it if necessary. Other ways to save money and find almost-new equipment at reduced prices are to check the buy, sell, and trade board in your local outfitting store or to browse at sales in the off season.

My equipment selection process usually involves a balance among six basic criteria: (1) cost, (2) protection from the cold, (3) protection from water, (4) weight, (5) durability, and (6) simplicity. Ask yourself these questions: How much does it cost? Will it help protect me from the cold? Will it hold up in the rain or after traveling through a stream? How much does it weigh? How durable is it? How simple is it in construction and operation, or can it be easily used and repaired? Notice carefully that all these, except the first, involve my well-being, comfort, and good times on the trail and can be applied to almost all equipment: boots, pack, clothing, shelter, and tools.

BOOTS

Your two most important pieces of equipment are going to be your boots, so don't scrimp in time or money spent in selecting them. A good pair of hiking boots, with the proper care, should last some years and be worth the price. The quality of the rest of the backpacking gear is not as important, but if your feet are blistered, bruised, or in some other way injured, you obviously can't walk; and if you can't walk, you can't backpack. So spend some time researching and fitting, and get good comfortable hiking boots. Walking any distance with or without fifty pounds on your back requires comfortable, but strong, support.

Boots are normally classified as to weight—from extremely lightweight walking boots, to hiking boots, to climbing boots. I recommend the hiking boot because it has more support than the lightest varieties, and you'll need that support when carrying a pack. The added weight on your back will cause you to come down more heavily than normal on your foot, and you don't want the boot to give and allow your ankle to twist. You'll also be walking across sharp rocks and through water, so the boot must be well made. Make sure that the upper of the boot is stitched to the sole; if it is only glued the boot will shortly begin to fall apart.

In the past I have consistently used Vibram soles because they don't skid readily on rocks and slippery surfaces. However, I have recently heard that this type of sole may be damaging to trails because it has a tendency to pick up large amounts of soil and thus aids erosion. So I am presently looking into other types of soles as possible alternatives.

Fitting Suggestions

My experience has been that if the boot doesn't feel basically comfortable in the store, it probably won't get any more comfortable in the next 100 or 500 miles. You should try boots on wearing the kind or kinds of socks (as to thickness) you plan to wear backpacking. I strongly recommend that you wear two pairs of socks while hiking. Therefore, when you try on your boots either (1) wear one pair of heavy wool Ragg socks; if the boots fit and feel good and comfortable, buy them one half size larger; or (2) wear one pair of heavy wool Ragg socks and one lighter pair of wool or cotton socks; if the boots fit and feel good and comfortable, buy them.

With whatever sock combination you prefer, you should be able to put your first finger between your heel and the back of the boot when your toes are touching the front. When the boot is laced for use, your heel should not lift more than one sixteenth to one eighth of an inch when you walk. Be sure that the boot is not too wide: your foot should not move when you twist your foot but should remain comfortably snug. You should be able to wiggle your toes when the boot is laced up.

Choosing a pair of boots is a subjective, personal process, so take your time, ask your friends, read about boots, try several different varieties, go to several different stores, and don't feel guilty about going back again and again if necessary.

Breaking In

Once you've bought a pair of hiking boots, you've got to break them in—long before you decide to take them on a trip. Being a "tenderfoot" is not fun. To break in the boots, take short walks to begin with, and then increase the distance, as rapidly as you like. You can wear them around the house and yard, to class, to work, but wear them. Finally, take a few short hikes in them with some weight on your back. This is the only true test of how comfortable the boots will be on the trail. Make sure that you fully break them in before a backpacking trip. Only you can tell when your boots are broken in, but, for example, my last pair had approximately 105 miles on them before I relied on them for trail work.

Seam sealer or wax should be placed in the crack between the sole and the side of the boot. Photo by Emil Ghinger.

To help break in your boots and to help prolong their life, you should treat them with care. Read the care instructions that come with the boots and follow them; if you don't, they are not going to last anywhere near their intended lifespan. The two things that will ruin your boots the fastest are water and excessive heat. Heat will dry the leather and make it crack, and water will seep in between the stitches and tend to rot the threads.

Since you can't keep your boots dry on a trip, it is important that they get the proper treatment at home. Before you leave, give them a heavy coating of good leather sealer or wax, whichever is recommended for your particular boot. Be sure to fill in the gap between the sole and the side of the boot with the sealer, so that no water will seep in through the seam. Take extra wax or sealer on the trail to treat your boots as needed. When you return home, dry and clean them thoroughly and treat them with wax once more.

OTHER CLOTHING

Taste in clothing is a very personal thing. Since I prefer natural fibers next to my body, I choose my clothes from wool or cotton materials or, for extreme warmth, from down covered with lightweight nylon. Here are the advantages and disadvantages of each of these materials:

Wool breathes (allows the natural passage of air through it) but is slightly heavier and more bulky than down. Most wools will shed moderate amounts of water; even when wet, though becoming heavier, they still remain good insulators from the cold.

Cotton breathes. It is relatively lightweight (lighter than wool), but usually not waterproof or water repellent unless it has been treated. Cotton can be easily washed and dried, an advantage when on the trail.

Down, pound for pound, is much lighter and warmer than wool and is the most effective insulation available when it's *dry*. Should it become wet, it's cold, heavy, and not much good for anything. It is harder to care for than wool or cotton, since it must be fluffed up in a dryer after being cleaned.

As of this date, several man-made fabrics have been developed which you may want to try:

Gore-tex (actually Teflon) — the "second generation" variety is not only wind repellent and breathable (the moisture inside is allowed to evaporate and escape) but is also completely waterproof. This generation of Gore-tex is less subject that its predecessor to any water leakage due to soiling. The fabric is used in such things as vests, parkas, sleeping bags, tents, rain ponchos, and lightweight hiking boots. It is relatively expensive but works very well.

fiber pile — a polyester fiber pile fabric; its makers claim it to be cheaper and lighter than wool and also to have better thermal insulating capacity when wet than wool. Used in clothing.

"Thinsulate" (trade name) — an insulative material claiming to provide twice the thermal resistance found in its competitive materials i.e. down, fiberfill, pile, or wool. It also breathes and absorbs less than 1 percent of its weight in water, thus retaining its insulative capacity even when wet.

You really don't need very many clothes on a camping trip, so here is a good place to cut down on weight. I take two pairs of pants (I'm wearing one) — one pair of 100 percent cotton (green or brown) pants and one pair of cotton-denim bluejeans. The extra pair is a good idea in case one set of clothes gets wet. I also take three shirts: one of cotton jersey for inner wear (long-sleeved or short-sleeved), one lightweight long-sleeved cotton shirt, and one wool shirt for outer wear. To this combination, I add a down vest (or a light parka if I'm going into the high mountains), a wool crusher hat (a brimmed, 100 percent wool hat that can be crushed or folded enough to fit into your pocket), a cotton fishnet undershirt (for added warmth), a bandanna (hair-tier-backer, sweat absorber, and potholder), and a belt.

Good socks are especially important and are the only clothing that you really need in some quantity. There is a good chance that some of your socks will get wet, and you want to have a dry pair to change into. I take a minimum of four pairs. I recommend that you wear two pairs at a time because sweat soaks through the inner pair to the outer pair and your feet stay dry. Make sure that you buy good ones; wool is recommended, but cotton will do nicely as well. And be sure that the thickness of your various sock combinations stays approximately consistent from change to change so your boots will always fit the same way. An extra pair of socks can also serve as mittens if you run into cold weather.

I also take a lightweight poncho in case of rain. Make sure you buy a good one with grommets (little metal-rimmed holes) around the sides so that, if need be, it can double as a tent tarp or emergency bivouac (tube tent). If you're going to pack into a rain forest during the rainy season, you may want to invest in nylon rain chaps. However, if the weather is at all warm while you're hiking, these are hot. Also, through sweat and condensation, your pants will probably end up just as wet as if you hadn't bothered with the chaps.

The lightweight poncho should have strong metal grommets and should be secured with a heavy-duty nylon rope. Photo by Emil Ghinger.

Again, don't take too many clothes, especially warm clothes. You will get hot walking with a pack, even in cool weather, and will need less clothing than you might think. A down vest and a wool shirt, a 60-40 jacket (60 percent two-ply cotton and 40 percent nylon), or a light parka, should be plenty for nights in camp, unless you are going on a winter trip.

I do allow myself one piece of clothing that is a luxury item. It feels particularly good to remove those hiking boots when you're settling down in camp and put lightweight shoes on your feet. I always make this weight allowance and take either trail moccasins or my running shoes, either of which is perfect. They're lightweight and sturdy and have good support. While you're relaxing, it's a good idea to dry your hiking boots a bit and get them ready for tomorrow's adventures — but not too close to the fire!

BACKPACKS

Backpacks come in about forty to sixty different styles, from small day packs to monstrosities that only mules should have to carry. The choice is yours, but remember that *you* have to carry it and that your pack should be not only comfortable but also practical.

It's important to have adequate padding on the shoulder straps and hip belt because unpadded straps will cut into your shoulders and hips when you are carrying a lot of weight. If you are interested in your pack lasting a while, make sure it's made of very strong nylon, which should be almost tear-resistant and definitely waterproof because, of necessity, packs take a beating. It should also be double or triple stitched with some kind of synthetic thread because cotton thread rots very quickly.

I always use a pack with a frame as opposed to a soft pack or a frame-less pack when I'm on a trip of any length and carrying more than twenty pounds. I have found that the frame ensures more comfortable traveling with heavier loads. It does this by a more efficient transfer of the weight in the pack to the hips and legs. This ensures better balance because the center of gravity is lower since the weight of the pack is supported lower in the body.

A soft pack may appear more comfortable than a pack with a frame when you first try it on because it is less bulky. However, I have found that it does not shift the weight from the shoulders to the hips very efficiently and will produce fatigue in a shorter time than will a pack with a frame. If you decide to use a soft pack, you must load it very carefully, making sure that no sharp or hard objects are going to push against your back. Fill the pack to capacity, thereby creating a sort of internal frame with the load. Again, I do not recommend soft packs for hikes longer than one day.

After you've tried the pack on – right in the store – put some weight in the pack and try it on again. Try adjusting the straps and the hip belt; remember that about 75 percent of the weight of the pack should fall on your hips, transferred there by the frame via the hip belt. This is a good reason for having the belt adequately padded. The shoulder straps should pick up the rest of the weight and guide the pack, which should be snug but not tight, shifting with your body and becoming a part of

Medium-sized frame pack with double compartments and upper and lower side pockets. Note the canteen positioned for hiking. Photo by Emil Ghinger.

it as you walk. Every person is built a little differently, so be sure that the pack you pick *can* be adjusted to fit *you* comfortably.

I carry a medium-sized frame pack with a double compartment because this eliminates my having to dig through the entire pack for something I need. This is especially true on the first few days out; after that you will know the approximate whereabouts of most things in your pack. It also has upper and lower pockets on the sides and back, which are a must. My pack and frame weigh between three and four pounds when empty.

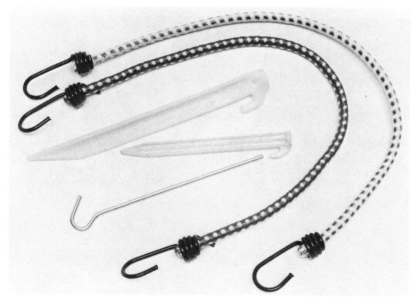

Shock-cord grapple hooks and three types of tent pegs—two plastic and one metal. Photo by Emil Ghinger.

I also take along a small, lightweight, inexpensive day pack for day excursions from camp. It's a wonderful feeling, after packing twenty, thirty, or forty miles in, to leave all your heavy gear in camp and take supplies for a one-day side trip to go exploring, animal watching, or whatever. This small pack is also the ideal thing for carrying wild foods, such as berries, back to camp.

One additional item will make packing your gear a lot easier. *Shock-cord grapple hooks* are indispensable accessories. Take one or two to fasten your tent, ground mat, and/or sleeping bag to the pack frame.

SHELTER

One of the physical pleasures and one of the most enjoyable parts of backpacking is sleeping outdoors, inhaling lots of fresh air, seeing the stars, and feeling snug in your bag while listening to the noises of

A lightweight poncho can be used as a tent tarp or to protect the pack from rain. Photo by Emil Ghinger.

the wilderness night. But this wonderful experience can turn into a miserable one if you don't plan your shelter well.

The choice of portable shelter varies with the individual. You may want to use as little shelter as possible; some people do not like to carry a tent but prefer to string a line between two trees or poles and construct a tube tent from a piece of plastic or their ponchos. Or they just sling their ponchos over a downed evergreen (a good windbreak shelter) or a clump of bushes and crawl under. I often just roll my bag out on the ground or in a sheltered spot, crawl in, and sleep under the stars. You will have problems, especially in the spring and summer in the East, with the heavy dew, so it's a good idea to cover your sleeping bag with your poncho. You can now purchase waterproof sleeping-bag covers for this purpose.

Tent

If you're going to go any distance and you're not into pure survival camping—for example, finding or making natural shelters along the way—the tent is your best protection and shelter. If you run into a lot of rain, severe cold, mosquitoes, or black flies, and you want to sit the inconvenience out, which is often the case, a tent is pure luxury. It allows you a small, dry, warm, or at least warmer, area, as well as a place to eat without being eaten, a refuge in which to wait for the weather to pass.

The selection of a tent, like the selection of most of the other outdoor equipment these days, will drive you nearly crazy from too many choices—at least it does me. However, as in the other cases, applying my criteria (cost, protection from cold and water, weight, durability, and simplicity) seems to help. A tent will be a costly item. Cheaply made ones are usually not worth buying because they don't breathe properly, aren't very durable, and wear out quickly. As I mentioned before, though, to save money you can always look for a good second-hand one or make one from a kit.

Backpacking tents are made of various types of nylon to ensure that they are lightweight. A tent for two people should not weigh more than about seven pounds. Make sure that the floor and the lowest six inches of the walls are made of heavy coated nylon. The heavier material keeps sharp rocks and other objects from puncturing the floor, and the coating keeps water from seeping through the floor during a heavy rain. The first time you set up your tent you may want to coat the seams with a seam sealer to ensure that it is absolutely waterproof. The walls of the tent should be made of ripstop nylon, which breathes, thereby preventing the build-up of heavy condensation in the tent. Both ends of the tent should be made of, or at least have vents made of, mosquito netting for adequate ventilation; you'll need that ventilation even in the cold of winter. A rain fly made of coated nylon protects the tent from rain. This fly may come attached to the tent at the top seam or it may be an entirely separate piece. Make sure that the tent you choose is made of flame-resistant fabrics.

Before you go into the woods, practice setting up your tent in the yard and sleep in it a few times. Be sure you are familiar with it and can put it up easily—you may have to in a blinding rain or windstorm. You don't want to be struggling with wind or swatting flies while trying to understand the pitching instructions.

I use two large plastic pegs for the front and rear mainstays and short plastic pegs or the metal screw pegs that usually come with the tent for the remainder. I have found that the metal screw pegs are slightly heavier, bend easily when you try to drive them into hard ground, and are more easily lost because of their dull color. As a matter of fact, I think I've found at least one tent peg somewhere on every trip. I always carry about 100 feet of nylon rope (one eighth to one fourth-inch in diameter), which serves as spare tent-stay line.

When you are on the trail, dry your tent in the open air. Before you store it at home, make sure it is absolutely dry or it will mildew and the cotton around the zippers will rot. If your tent gets heavy use, after a while it will begin to leak around the seams and will need resealing with a tent seam sealer.

Sleeping Bag

There are so many variables concerning sleeping comfort that it's almost impossible to make a recommendation about sleeping bags. Your choice will depend on such things as the season in which you plan to go camping, the area to which you are going, whether or not you wear clothes to sleep in, what's between your bag and the ground, whether or not you're in a tent and protected from the wind, and your own body's metabolism or heat-generating capacity. When you enter the store, you will be confronted by many different types and brands as well as with six or eight different types of inner construction.

At this point, befuddled by visual and sensory overload, I revert to my six criteria and a little experience. For the first five or six years that I went backpacking, I carried an old green army mountain-arctic bag. (This is the duck-down kind you can still buy at army-navy stores or pawn shops for about $20, and after sleeping in it, you wake up covered with feathers.) This was an excellent and durable, but heavy and bulky, bag. Then one day, with the leaks getting worse, I got tired of carrying the extra weight—a pound or two—and simultaneously ran into someone who needed some money very badly. So I bought my first nylon, goose-down sleeping bag. It is a middle-weight bag (approximately three to four pounds) supposedly to be used during spring, summer, and fall; the tag also said to $-10°$ F. I've found that it is a little too hot in a tent without my clothes in the late spring, summer, and early fall in low areas where the nights are mild. For higher areas—sleeping in a tent without clothes—where the nights are colder, it is about right. However, this is my personal experience; you must experiment for yourself because you will surely find things a little different.

Some people now use a combination bag—a fiberfill and down bag. It has polyester fiberfill on the bottom and down on the top. The reasoning is that down, when on the bottom side of bags, becomes compressed by the weight of the sleeper. Without fluff and air space, down doesn't keep you warm, and you begin to shiver. The fiberfill is as lightweight as the down and stuffs well (fits easily into a "stuff sack" for carrying); it also maintains its loft (becomes compacted less readily) and therefore supposedly keeps you warmer on the bottom. The down on the top of the bag, meanwhile, doesn't become compressed because it's not bearing any weight; theoretically, you're warmer all over.

My recommendation is, except for midwinter backpacking and high-altitude expeditions, to go simple and light. Try a spring-summer-fall down or down and fiberfill combination bag (total weight—three to four pounds). This type of bag will provide the widest range for sleeping comfort, will give you the most use of your bag, and is by no means the most expensive choice. I can promise you that if you go overboard on the down—if you buy the "Denali-Himalayan-Alpine-Mountaineering Expedition Whole-Goose-Flock-Feather Special"—good only for climbing Mt. McKinley or Mt. Everest—you will wake up in the night and find yourself in a pool of sweat.

Between trips, air out the bag thoroughly and hang it up in a dry place instead of keeping it crushed in its bag. This will ensure that the down retains its loft as long as possible. If your down sleeping bag gets wet, don't dry it in front of an intense heat source such as a campfire. The heat from the fire will make the down clump together and ruin the bag. Instead, hang it on a line in the sun or, if you are at home, put it in a dryer on *low* with a couple of tennis balls to help fluff it up.

Ground Mat

If you're cold you can't relax, and you'll wake up more fatigued than when you went to sleep. One of the most important factors in warm sleeping is what's between you (your bag) and the ground. You actually need more insulation under you than on top of you because the ground is a better heat conductor than the air. Thus the ground mat, or whatever you use for ground cover, is every bit as important as

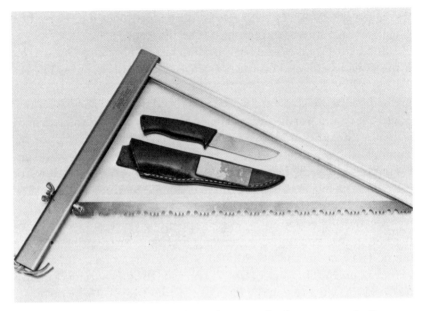

Knife with 5-inch blade, a small Carborundum stone for sharpening, and a Sven-saw. Photo by Emil Ghinger.

the bag. This ground cover insulates you, preventing the rapid transfer of your body heat to the colder ground. It also keeps moisture from seeping into the bag.

To me it seems cumbersome and incongruous to go into the wilderness carrying an air mattress or a two-inch-thick urethane mattress, both of which weigh two pounds. I carry the lightest, most functional item I've found—a three-eighths- or one-fourth-inch-thick, shoulder-to-knee (24×48, standard size), Ensolite or polyethylene foam pad, which weighs approximately one half pound or less. This is much lighter and also warmer than the two items mentioned above.

OTHER EQUIPMENT AND ACCESSORIES

Knife. A knife is probably the most versatile tool you will have on your trip, so get a good one. You will use it for everything from cleaning fish to making kindling. I carry a good quality, light, high-grade steel hunting knife with a sheath. This knife's blade is extremely durable and hard, holds an edge for a long time, and is resistant to corrosion and rust. A five-inch blade should be sufficient for your needs. Also tuck a small (approximately 1 × 3 × ⅜ inch) carborundum stone in a pocket of your pack. This stone weighs only an ounce and a half, and with a little practice, you will be able to use it to keep your knife very sharp.

Here, very briefly, is how to sharpen your knife. Before leaving on a trip, saturate the stone with oil (penetrating or household oil). Holding the knife edge nearly flat against the stone, but at a slight angle, move the knife toward the cutting edge. Use almost straight, even strokes, not circular ones. Sharpen each side of the knife blade the same amount (use the same number of strokes).

Map (covered completely in the Orientation section). Try to get a topographic map of the general area in which you are going to hike. If possible, I make a point of obtaining a copy well before the trip. It helps a lot in general planning. You can obtain government topographic maps in outfitting stores or bookstores. In Canada the government information offices and provincial offices stock maps. To obtain U.S. maps, if you live east of the Mississippi River, write: Distribution Section, U.S. Geologic Survey, Washington, D.C. 20242. If you live west of the Mississippi River, write: Distribution Section, USGS, Denver, CO 80225. If you live in Alaska, write: Distribution Section, USGS, 301 First Ave., Fairbanks, AK 99701.

Compass (covered completely in the Orientation section). The Swedes and Germans make good, light, relatively inexpensive models. The important thing is that you know how to *use* it.

Waterproof match box. Any outdoor store will have one of these inexpensive items. It's important that you make sure that it is filled with matches that work *before* going on a trip. For extra insurance, you may want to take a supply (one box) of waterproof matches.

Canteen. I carry a standard two-quart aluminum special in a cloth case with a long strap. I hang the canteen on the outside of my pack, between the top of the two pack-frame poles. The canteen can't fall off

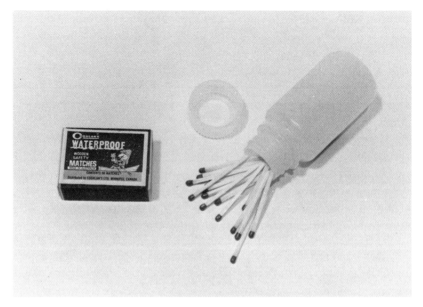

A waterproof match container and a box of waterproof matches. Photo by Emil Ghinger.

and is easily accessible. If you are going to an area that does not have a readily available water supply, be sure to take water containers (full!) — at least a *quart* of water for each person for each day you will be out.

Fishing lines and hooks. I make up a small packet of three or four medium-sized fishhooks and ten to thirty yards of six- to ten-pound-test nylon line. I tape the hooks and line between two pieces of scrap leather thick enough so the fishhooks can't penetrate it. If you carry an emergency fishing kit and you decide to stay out for a few more days, or if the "raccoon platoon" gets into your food, with some luck you'll have fish to eat.

Stones or small rocks make good sinkers, if you need them. Worms, grubs, frogs, crayfish, and especially aquatic insects are good wild baits. Watch what the fish are eating and try to use the same thing. After catching your first fish, open its stomach to find out what it has been eating. Then, if you can obtain that particular insect or whatever it is, you know you've got good bait. Sometimes you can re-use baits found in the stomachs of fish or try a small piece of fish itself.

Insect repellent and mosquito head-net. Insect repellent, from my experience, works better if it stinks and is greasy, and though nothing works indefinitely, it does help. I use a repellent called "Old Woodsman's Fly Dope," or just "Fly Dope." I don't use the other commercial insect repellents because I really don't like to use any product on my skin that has cautions all over the label. Besides, I've tried the other top brands, and the Fly Dope, though it stinks strongly of the inside of an old stovepipe (it's made of such things as vinegar, menthol, camphor, creosote juice, and some fat), works as well if not better than anything else I have tried. An apparently very effective insect repellent was prepared by the Kickapoo Indians by taking a small amount of bear oil (bear grease) and mixing it with crushed Ohio buckeye leaves. The bark of this tree is well known for its "stink."

I also pack a mosquito head-net. If you happen to be out at the height of black-fly season or when the mosquitoes are hatching, you will greatly appreciate this item. A head-net will allow you to set up your tent and enjoy your meal in peace. It's a good idea to make this netting so that it fits over your hat's brim (a brimmed hat because if the netting rests on your head and isn't held out from your face, they're gonna get you) and comes down and rests on your shoulders with plenty of netting to spare. This loose fit enables you to move head and body without losing your cover. If you don't want to make it or don't already have a favorite hat, you can buy the net and hat or just the net from an outdoor store or catalog.

The items I've listed are the most important equipment. You could, with a little survival knowledge, "make it" without any of them. Since I'm out to enjoy the outdoors and not to worry about survival, these are the first things I check for in my pack before walking down the trail. But again, the most important thing is that you know how to use each piece of equipment effectively. The following items are not really necessary but are very handy, and I've used them many times in the woods.

Saw. I used to carry my old Boy Scout hatchet on backpacking trips, but I've discovered that a far more valuable tool, at approximately half the weight (one instead of two pounds), is the aluminum Sven-saw. It assembles into a right triangle with a twenty-inch sawing blade. When it is not in use, it can be folded into a long, thin rectangular shape (1 ×

Most backpacking stoves are very reliable in all climates and at all altitudes. This model retails for about $55. Photo by Emil Ghinger.

1½ × 20 inches), which straps nicely to the side or bottom of your pack. I used to use the back of my hatchet for a hammer, but rocks or a piece of dead wood cut into club length by the saw are always available for pounding in tent pegs or other tasks. Besides, even in the best of hands, an axe or hatchet is much more dangerous than a saw.

Cookstove. I used to consider a backpacking stove a luxury to be used only during very windy or rainy conditions. However, there are many hiking areas, such as the Appalachian Trail in the eastern United States, where campfires are now prohibited because of high risk of forest fires, overuse of the trail systems, and scarcity of firewood. Thus the backpacking stove, fueled by white gas, kerosene, butane, or alcohol, is rapidly becoming a necessity. If you are planning to camp in a national or state park, forest, or trail system, write ahead to find out whether you will need to bring a stove.

Most of the ten or fifteen models of campstoves are well made, durable, and quite reliable—*if used and cared for properly.* In outfitting

This stove—the Svea 123R—retails for about $40. Photo by Emil Ghinger.

stores and equipment catalogs, you will find advantages and disadvantages, ratings and comparisons according to fuels, weights, use at various altitudes, boiling times, burning times, temperatures, and heating capacities!

One of the main considerations is *weight*—the weight of the stove and, don't forget, the weight of the fuel and the fuel container. The smaller backpacking stoves weigh approximately a pound and a half, cost about $40, and, folded up, are about the size of your mess kit. The steel or aluminum fuel container and the fuel in it will add another one or two pounds depending on the size of the container.

I have used three models, all small, simple, and adequate. One, the *Optimus 8R*, a white-gas burner that weighs 1¾ pounds, is self-cleaning and requires no pumping (priming); another, the *Svea 123R*, a white-gas burner that weighs 1⅛ pounds, is also self-cleaning and requires no pumping; and the third, the *Optimus 00*, is a kerosene burner that you have to clean (comes equipped with little cleaning pins) and pump. It weighs 1⅝ pounds. I think all three of these stoves are light, compact, relatively safe, and stable.

I do recommend, however, that before purchasing any model, you try to talk to someone who has used it. (The people working in the outfitting stores are sometimes good sources.) Also, before using the stove, read the operating instructions and cautions very carefully. Then use the stove several times and make sure you understand how it works *before* you take it on a trip. Why? Because all of the fuels except kerosene —that is, white gas, butane, and alcohol—are *extremely* volatile, especially when under pressure, as they are in backpacking stoves. If used improperly, all three are dangerous. For this reason, of the backpacking stoves I've used (even though I have to clean the orifice and pump it), I like the kerosene Optimus 00 best. Kerosene also will not ignite as readily if spilled and is easier to obtain than the other fuels.

Problems that you may encounter with a backpacking stove include clogged orifices, pressure leaks, priming difficulties, and overheating. However, you can avoid these problems by using the stove according to the directions in a place with adequate air circulation, and, most importantly, by keeping your stove clean, especially the fuel orifice. In the models with a built-in cleaning pin, you have only to activate the pin several times before lighting the stove; in the others you have to remove the little head or nipple and push the pin through the fuel orifice. Just to make sure, I always blow through the orifice. Always clean the stove thoroughly after using it on a trip. Empty the fuel from the stove before you put it away. All these volatile fuels, including kerosene, "gum up" or "break down" when exposed to air over a period of time, which can impair the working parts of the stove. Keep the stove stored where dust and dirt can't get into it.

Instead of using any of these liquid-fuel stoves, I now carry a little solid-fuel backpacking stove because it is cheap, lightweight, easy to pack, and, most importantly, cannot malfunction, leak, or explode. It also has no disposable parts. (I have found empty fuel containers for butane gas stoves in very remote areas.) The stove I use is an ingenious little device put out by Esbit. It costs about $2 or $3 at most. The sides to the little metal box open halfway to heat liquids right in an aluminum pack cup, or open fully to accommodate the liter or quart container of the mess ket. This little device, like the other stoves, boils water in minutes and will nicely fry a fresh fish if necessary. The fuel-tablet box fits neatly inside the closed rectangular box for storage, and the whole thing weighs five to eight ounces. I usually carry, depending on the length of the trip, one or two extra boxes of tablets. Meta makes two other solid-fuel models, model numbers 71 and 80, which are slightly larger. They are also self-contained units and weigh four ounces and eight ounces, respectively.

Whether you decide to use the liquid, gas, or solid-fuel stove is a matter of personal preference, depending on the number of people on the trip and the amount and types of food you take with you. I prefer the safety, simplicity, reliability, and economy of the solid-fuel models.

Utensils. I keep this department as simple as possible. Since you are already carrying a knife, there isn't much reason to duplicate it in the mess kit or in a separate utensil kit. Forks are especially useless, excess weight. Anything that can be eaten with a fork can also be eaten with a spoon, but the reverse is not true. (Ever try to eat soup with a fork?) If you decide that you really need a fork, it's easy to make one: cut and sharpen the two prongs on a dead forked branch. The point of your hunting knife is a readymade fork substitute. Two small, peeled sticks make excellent chopsticks. The only eating utensils I take are small wooden spoons because they weigh less than metal, won't burn your hand if you forget them over the fire for a minute, are much more durable than plastic, and if lost in the woods will deteriorate naturally. My bandanna serves as a potholder.

I carry a standard, cheap, nesting mess kit, which includes a one-quart sauce pot, frying pan, deep plate, and plastic drinking cup. I have removed the cup and carry a much more versatile variety (see below). The mess kit weighs about one pound. However, if your cooking is more

A Sierra cup and wooden spoons. A bandanna can be used as a potholder. Photo by Emil Ghinger.

elaborate and you don't mind carrying the extra weight, you may want to invest in some other kind or combination of the numerous cook sets, kettles, cups, and pans that are now offered. You can probably find cheaper varieties in army-navy stores than in the camping stores. I have found that one simple cooking kit suffices quite nicely on the trail for two people.

I carry a Sierra cup instead of the plastic cup that comes with the mess kit. They're made of "indestructo" stainless steel, have sturdy wire handles, and weigh three ounces. I especially like to carry one because I can hang it from a loop on the outside of my pack, ready to dip water from a spring. If I want hot chocolate, tea, or coffee, the water can be heated very quickly directly *in the cup* – no need to get out the mess kit.

Zip-lock plastic bags. Almost all of my food – the trail mixes, granola, cereal grains and flours, dried fruits, dried milk, powdered eggs, and energy ration-bars – is packaged in these. The tops pinch tightly together and usually stay that way, keeping moisture and bugs out and

A nesting mess kit can save valuable space. Photo by Emil Ghinger.

food in. They're also good for other small items you want to keep dry. Be careful about filling them too full (two thirds is about right) because the tops do tend to pop open if the bags are overloaded. The wire closers of regular plastic bags usually rip the bag tops, and sooner or later you have a mess.

Refillable poly-tubes. I'm also an advocate of these small (weight one ounce) plastic tubes, which are ideal for carrying honey, maple syrup,

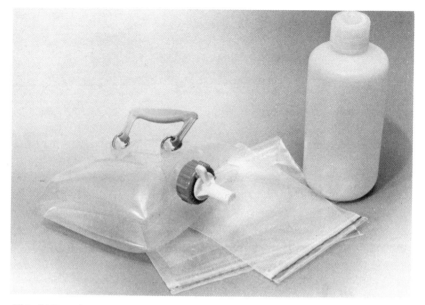

This folding plastic water container can hold up to 1 gallon. Zip-lock plastic bags are used to hold dried fruits, powdered eggs, and the like. Plastic bottle can be used as a substitute canteen. Photo by Emil Ghinger.

jams, nut butters, or anything else that is spreadable and sticky. Here again, make sure you don't overfill the tubes (two thirds is sufficient) and make sure the pin-clip arrangement that seals the bottom of the tube is properly fitted, or you'll have a mess.

Metal or plastic film containers. These containers, which you get free when you buy many types of camera film, weigh almost nothing, have tight-fitting tops, and are excellent for carrying spices and condiments.

Water container. I always take a plastic folding container with at least a one-gallon capacity (weight three ounces). It also comes in a bucket variety (weight six ounces). Why a water container? Because if you've found a beautiful campsite 100 or 200 feet on a rise above a river or lake and you've just returned in the late afternoon from a long hike, one trip to the water source—for drinking, cooking, and washing—till the next morning is plenty.

These containers are all that I usually take, but small to large lightweight containers for just about any kind of food, liquid, or condiment are available—from moisture-proof salt and pepper shakers to all kinds of fuel bottles, squirt bottles, or flasks. Don't bother to buy too many special containers in a fancy backpacking store. Try plastic containers you have at home. Some of them will do just as nicely. Do not take *glass* into the wilderness; it has been the cause of more than one forest fire.

Other items that I like to have along and that are well worth the weight to me include the following.

Heavy-duty nylon rope. I carry approximately 50 to 100 feet of one-eighth- to one-quarter-inch diameter nylon rope. This comes in handy for extra tent stays, roping hikers together on very steep, narrow trails, hand guide-rope while crossing a creek on a fallen log (provided you're good at throwing a lariat!), dragging heavy objects such as logs, tying packs between trees to keep animals out of them, and a hundred other uses you'll discover for yourself.

Thin-gauge copper wire. A couple of feet of thin-gauge copper wire (copper because it bends easily without breaking and is strong) for simple repair of things such as packs and mess kit handles.

Biodegradable camp soap. I take a small tube or bottle of biodegradable camp soap. The best one I've found is called "Coughlan's Plus 50 Sportsman's Soap," which is liquid concentrated coconut oil soap. It smells good, works even better, and there's no chance of polluting rivers, streams, or lakes.

Small sewing kit. This consists of one small spool of heavy-duty thread, one small spool of regular polyester thread, two sewing needles, and a few assorted safety pins, straight pins, and buttons.

Small pocket flashlight or candle. You'll need a small light, backpacking light and/or candle for the night. I use artificial light as little as possible in the woods. If you give your eyes a chance, they will adjust to the darkness. However, I do take along a flashlight in case of emergency.

Luxuries. This category includes a camera, binoculars, backpacking rod and reel, and writing and sketching materials. I consider all of these to be optional. Remember that you are going to be conscious of every extra pound in your backpack. The added enjoyment you get from these items may not be worth the struggle of taking them along.

FIRST-AID KIT

The contents of my first-aid kit vary depending on the length of my trip and the region to which I'm going. For short trips (up to a week) where I'm within several hours of a telephone, telegraph, or house, I usually leave most of my kit behind. For more extended trips, where I'm several days' travel from any communications, I take the whole kit. Here again, the most important thing is that *you* have a basic knowledge of first aid and can wisely use what you have in your kit. Basic first aid is neither mysterious nor complicated. I don't think there's really any substitute for a good basic course in first aid, but there is one book that I reread every time before I head off for a month or so. It's called *Being Your Own Wilderness Doctor* by E. R. Kodet and Bradford Angier.

My complete first-aid kit contains the following:

1 good pair of tweezers — invaluable for splinters, prickers, and many other small things.

1 pair of surgical scissors — for cutting bandages, tape, etc.

1 finger splint — mine is made of foam-backed aluminum, but you can just as easily carry some tongue depressors or split a piece of wood and use its flat side.

Butterfly closures — five or six, used to hold wounds together. (I use them in place of suturing because it's much simpler.)

Bandages and Band-aids — some of various sizes and shapes.

1 large (4 × 4) emulsion-coated bandage — for serious burns.

4 × 4 surgical dressings — for covering cuts, lacerations, and wounds.

Ammonia inhalants — one package of two for reviving an unconscious person.

1 small roll of sterile gauze dressing — for wrapping bandages on cuts, wounds, etc.

8 × 8 piece of adhesive moleskin — for blister treatment or prevention.

1 small vial of talcum powder — for foot lubrication or treatment of crotch abrasion.

1 roll of surgical tape — for taping bandages and moleskin in place. I much prefer this to adhesive tape because it's much thinner, lighter, and easier to use.

1 Ace bandage — for wrapping twisted joints, ankles, torn muscles. If you don't have one along, you can easily tear or cut up an article of clothing or use your bandanna or strips of bark in an emergency.

1 tube Chapstick — for chapped or parched lips, to prevent splitting and bleeding.

1 small bottle of aspirin — (50–75 tablets) for headaches, reducing fevers associated with infection, pain associated with sore muscles, teeth, etc.

* *1 small bottle of aspirin with codeine* — for more severe pain.
* *1 small bottle Benadryl or pyribenzamine* — antihistamine for colds, allergic reactions associated with sinusitus, insect bites, poison oak, ivy, etc.
* *1 small bottle of Lomotil or bismuth paregoric tablets* — for diarrhea.
* *1 bottle pro-Banthine* — (25–30 tablets), used to settle stomach spasms or cramps usually associated with severe vomiting or diarrhea.
* *1 bottle of Compazine* — (12–15 tablets) for extreme nausea, vomiting, dry heaving.
* *1 bottle Pyridium* — (15–20 tablets.) If you've ever had a urinary tract infection or cystitis, chances are you know about this. It makes your urine orange but is an analgesic for the urinary tract that will allow you to urinate without pain or burning sensation. In the meantime you should start a sulfa drug or head for a doctor.
* *1 bottle Septra or Gantrisin* — (30 tablets) for urinary-tract infection.
* *Erythromycin, Vibramycin, or other broad-spectrum antibiotic* — (25–30 tablets) for infection.

1 small tube of Bacitracin antibiotic ointment — for covering wounds.

1 small tube of Spectrocin ointment — for infections or irritations of the eyes such as pink eye.

1 small tube of Tetracaine ointment — topical anesthetic for numbing the skin after, for example, severe insect bite.

1 small bottle of salt tablets — for maintaining the body's salt levels when sweating profusely in hot weather.

Snake-bite kit.

Oral thermometer.

You will need a prescription for all of the starred items. Talk with your doctor, tell him you are going hiking in a wilderness area, and ask him for prescriptions and directions for the use of these drugs. Make sure you understand thoroughly what you have: the symptoms, dosages, and contraindications. One more thing—I also make sure that if it's a controlled drug that I'm carrying the bottle label has *my* name on it. If you cross national borders on your trips, this will save you time and trouble with the border patrol.

2. Planning for the Trip

PHYSICAL CONDITIONING

Physical conditioning is something that should be considered *before* going on any trip or adventure where it will be, out of necessity, required. While backpacking, you have to carry not only yourself but also your pack while climbing hills and mountains, descending steep trails into valleys, and crossing streams and rivers. You will not have a very good time if you have to be concerned with chronic shortness of breath or if you simply can't go where you or others would like to go because you don't think you can physically make it.

My recommendation is this: Get yourself in relatively good shape before you go and you'll have a better time. If your life is extremely sedentary and you're in very bad physical shape and not used to exercise or if you are in some other way unhealthy, begin slowly and take it easy. You may not only discourage yourself but actually harm yourself by trying to get in shape too quickly. I think you can safely start with walking several miles on level ground, if need be. Then walk for longer times and distances and add some distance uphill. Increase the distance daily and then try a few higher hills. Then try jogging those first distances, or maybe even longer ones, to increase your lung capacity and improve your breathing techniques.

I don't want to discourage you at the start. Backpacking itself is an excellent means for getting into shape. No matter what condition you're in when you set off, you will undoubtedly be in much better shape after a few days of hiking. However, my concern for your physical condition is so that you'll enjoy those first few days on the trail and won't abandon backpacking after one attempt.

If you can't get yourself in shape beforehand, go anyway. It will be a little more painful, but the results will be astonishing. Walking ten to fifteen miles a day will tone you up faster than almost any other type of exercise.

CHECKLISTS

Before going on any backpacking trip, it is a good idea to make written checklists of all equipment, clothing, and food. As you gain experience, this will become easier and require very little time. Following are samples of my checklists, which you can use as a guide.

Equipment and Tools Checklist

Pack (with shock-cord grapple hooks)   _____
Sleeping bag   _____
Tent (with all pegs)
   or sheet of plastic for tube tent   _____
Ground mat   _____
Knife   _____
Map   _____
Compass   _____
Waterproof match container
   and/or matches   _____
First-aid kit   _____
Canteen   _____
Emergency fishing gear   _____
Mess kit   _____
Insect repellent and head-net   _____
Saw   _____
Stove and fuel   _____
Heavy-duty nylon rope   _____

Copper wire   _____
Small sewing kit   _____
Extra boot wax   _____
Plastic water container   _____
2 large plastic garbage bags   _____
Extra zip-lock bags   _____
Wooden spoons   _____
Day pack   _____

In addition to making this checklist, you should thoroughly check all the items listed for possible repair or replacement. The pan may be missing from your mess kit, one or more of the tent pegs may be missing, one of the tent lines may be frayed or a grommet may be tearing, or the zipper on your sleeping bag may be broken. The most important thing to check is the condition of your boots.

The failure of most equipment (good equipment) is not instantaneous but occurs rather gradually as the result of rugged use (even faster if it's rugged abuse) and is very noticeable even with the most cursory inspection. It's a good idea—it only takes a minute—to check before you go.

Clothing Checklist

Pants (2 pairs)   _____
Belt   _____
Light cotton shirt (long-sleeved)   _____
Cotton jersey undershirts (2)   _____
Wool shirt or lightweight jacket   _____
Wool crusher hat   _____
Socks (4 pairs)   _____
Hiking boots   _____
Camp shoes   _____
Rain poncho   _____
Down vest (or lightweight parka)   _____
Water purification tablets   _____
Toilet paper   _____

Optional:
Shorts or bathing suit   _____
Sweater (lightweight)   _____

Personal care checklist (optional as desired or shared
if possible to eliminate extra weight):
1 small towel   _____
Hairbrush or comb   _____
Toothbrush/paste   _____
Camp soap (biodegradable)   _____
Dental floss   _____
Sunglasses   _____

The contents of these lists obviously depend on when and where
you're planning to go, but I usually take much the same combination. I
try to cover most types of weather. During the summer, even when the
mountain valleys are hot, if you decide to hike up a mountain trail or
through a pass, it may be snowing. The clothing list is where I usually
lighten my load if I know I'm going to an area of specific terrain and
weather.

Complete Food Checklist

7-Day Suggested Menu

Breakfast	*Lunch*	*Dinner*
oatmeal with dried fruit	quickstart or trail mix raisins	bouillon or tomato soup
stickbread with cinnamon	energy ration-bar	garlic pan bread (wheat)
coffee, tea, or cocoa		scrambled eggs with onions and herbs
		rice pudding
		tea or cocoa
wheatcakes with wild or dried fruit, honey, or jam	quickstart or trail mix dried apricots or prunes	split-pea soup herbed pan bread hot corn cereal and
coffee, tea, or cocoa	energy ration-bar	cinnamon
		tea or cocoa
hot whole-wheat cereal	quickstart or trail mix dried peaches or pears	cream of mushroom soup

pan bread (onion)	energy ration-bar	cinnamon cornbread
coffee, tea, or cocoa		brown rice cooked with bouillon cubes
		tea or cocoa
dried-apple compote	dried figs or dates	tomato soup
cream of rice cereal or	with peanut butter	corncakes with dried
oatmeal with cin-	or quickstart or	fruit
namon and raisins	trail mix	quickstart cookies
coffee, tea, or cocoa	energy ration-bar	tea or cocoa
whole-wheat cereal or	quickstart or trail mix	chicken noodle soup
scrambled eggs	raisins	brown rice with
with onions	energy ration-bar	tomato sauce
pan bread with herbs		peanut butter and
coffee, tea, or cocoa		dates
corncakes or wheat	quickstart or trail mix	split-pea soup
cakes and wild or	dried apricots or pears	pan bread with
dried fruit with	or black mission	onions
honey, maple syrup,	figs	scrambled eggs with
or jam	energy ration-bar	herbs
coffee, tea, or cocoa		prune cobbler
		tea or cocoa
oatmeal and dried or	quickstart or trail mix	vegetable soup
wild fruit	prunes or dates	hot corn cereal with
stickbread with cin-	energy ration-bar	nuts
namon and jam		quickstart cookies or
coffee, tea, or cocoa		figs and sesame
		butter
		tea or cocoa

To any of the cereals, you can add a tablespoon of dried milk, any dried fruit or wild fruit, a handful of quickstart, any nuts you like, and sweetening to your taste. Remember, this is only a guide, and the possible variations and/or changes are almost infinite.

Try to organize your food roughly by meal and by day. This is obviously an approximation, but it helps so that you don't needlessly end up carrying twenty pounds too much food or end up with nothing to eat and two days left to pack out. Don't forget that a day *in* is very much equal to a day *out* in terms of food.

Overall, when planning, the most important consideration is to coordinate your equipment and tools, clothing, and food with the intended duration and destination of your backpacking trip.

HOW MUCH WEIGHT TO CARRY AND HOW TO PACK IT

How much weight is it feasible to carry on your back? This varies with the individual. The top weight that I can comfortably carry is about sixty pounds. I prefer a bit less; any more and I don't have good balance control on steep, narrow trails. I'm almost 6 feet tall, weigh a little less than 160 pounds, and am in good physical condition. A very rough estimate of how much weight you can comfortably carry is between one fourth and three eighths of your body weight. However, here's my test for the proper amount of weight: (1) pack up your pack, always putting the heaviest items in the lower sections because you want to keep your center of gravity as low as possible; (2) put the pack on, fasten the waist belt, and adjust the straps, if need be (see section on How to adjust your pack); (3) bend over and untie and retie your shoelace. If you can do this and still maintain good control, you will probably be able to maneuver your load safely. If you cannot do this, you'd better check through it again—it could be that some of the heavier items are packed too near the top and your center of gravity is too high or that you're over your weight limit. This checkup is important. If you have any doubts, leave out some items now or you will find yourself discarding them along the way. Happily, your pack will get a little lighter every day as you eat your food supplies.

OBTAINING MAPS

Once you've decided approximately where you want to go, it's a good idea to obtain maps of the area ahead of time. This helps in the planning stages and is very interesting; a good map can tell you a lot about the region before your arrival. The most reliable maps that I've found are topographic maps or good hiking-trail maps made expressly for that purpose. The topographic maps ("topos," for short) are usually available at any good outfitting store or bookstore. If you can't get them at one of these places, write to the USGS offices. (See p. 31 for complete addresses.)

If you're going into a national park in the United States or Canada, special, detailed topos of the park itself or of parts of it are usually available at the park ranger's headquarters or in the nearest town. I wouldn't count on being able to find them, though, especially at the height of the season.

NATURAL HOMEWORK

To have a much richer, more enjoyable time while backpacking, do a little investigative homework so you will know what to expect from a given area in the way of climate, topography, animal life, and plant life. Even a very limited amount of information and familiarity will make things much more interesting. This is also the best way to avoid the consequent "fear of the unknown," which you will be up against if things don't go according to plan and you get lost or find yourself in some other predicament. Imaginary dangers are frequently the chief source of worry. You must remember to rely on reason and *knowledge*.

You can obtain this information by talking with other people who have been near or in the same area you want to visit or by reading about it. There are excellent field guides, covering all parts of the United States and Canada, on every aspect of natural history from animal tracks to weeds. (See the selected readings at the end of Chapter 5.)

PRIOR NOTIFICATION OF DESTINATION AND DURATION; PERMITS

Before going into a wilderness area, whether it is a park or otherwise, it is a must to *notify* someone beforehand—friends at home, park rangers, the owner of the general store at the nearest crossroads—as to your approximate destination, route of travel, and estimated length of stay. Then, if you don't come back for some reason, they will either come looking for you, know enough to notify someone who will, or at least be able to give information and help to someone who has come looking for you. Please remember to check in with the people you notified when you return to civilization. Don't be the cause of a large search effort when you're sitting comfortably at home.

If you're going into a national or state park or into a controlled and patrolled wilderness area, assume that it is necessary to have some kind of permit. With the increased numbers of people using the wilderness areas, the parks are unfortunately forced to make more and more rules enforcing the proper usage of the lands. So you might need an open-fire permit or find out that you're restricted to building fires only in the provided fire containers. You'll probably also need a fishing license or permit if you want to fish.

This is also a good time to find out some information about where you're headed. The rangers can describe the trails to you, tell you what wildlife has been spotted lately, and, most importantly, give you information about trail conditions. For example, if it's early in the season after a hard winter, and you're in the Rockies, the pass to your lake may be still under ten feet of ice and snow. The people at park headquarters will know this because people are asked to report on the trail conditions, fishing, animal life, and so forth, of the area where they've been.

You can also tell them at this time where you're going and how long you'll be out. If it's late in the day, they should also be able to direct you to a good place nearby to camp for the night, so that you can get an early start the next morning.

PETS

I urge you to *leave your dog, cat, or monkey at home*, for several reasons. If you've brought your pet along, there's a good chance you won't see any wildlife because it'll be looking for the animals, too—100 yards ahead of you. Dogs and bears don't mix—a bear might kill your dog, or your dog might bring the bear back to your tent. Many parks don't allow pets, and you will be turned away. Pets, especially cats, may wander off and become lost, and they don't stand a good chance of surviving on their own in the wilderness.

I know it may be hard to leave your pet at home when it would obviously love the trip so much, *but please do so.* There are very few areas left in the United States that approach anything like natural conditions for wild animals, and it's not fair to disrupt these few relatively undisturbed, tranquil places.

3. Provisioning Your Pack

Deciding what food to take on the trail is obviously a matter of personal choice; what you will want to take depends on your regular diet. You will be incredibly hungry when you are backpacking in the wilds because of all the exercise and the appetite-stimulating influence of the outdoors, and food will become very important to you. You will especially crave high-energy foods—pack them and eat them and don't worry about proteins, vitamins, and minerals because you are not going to develop any deficiencies in the time you will be out. Besides, with the abundance of mental and physical healing powers of the outdoors— fresh air, sunshine, and good, pure water—it would be extremely difficult to impair your health in a week's time even if you ate *nothing!*

The most important considerations when planning your food are: (1) keeping weight to a minimum and (2) simplicity of preparation. The American Indian, when hunting on foot or on horseback, traveled hundreds of miles in a week's time, existing on a few pounds of cornmeal, jerky, or solidified bear fat, plus what wild berries and fruits could be easily foraged. Until you gain some experience in traveling in the woods, it is better to *travel light*. Carrying a supermarket on your back along with all your other gear can be exhausting, as well as discouraging. Exactly what you pack to eat is up to you; just be sure you can comfortably carry it!

Keep foods *simple*. Simple foods require little or no preparation. I recommend including lots of high-energy raw snacks that you can eat on the trail with no preparation. For example:

> They [the Indians] esteem it [bear fat] among the most valuable articles of food, especially in their journeys. It is highly nutritive, agrees well with the stomach, and produces no thirst. From the smallness of the quantity necessary to satisfy the appetite, it produces no shortness of breath. The Indians, while traveling, take about (4) four ounces in twenty-four hours, which they continue for days together, with very little other nourishment. (*Memoirs of a Captivity Among the Indians of North America*, John Dunn Hunter, p. 90)

There are many foods besides bear fat that ensure a good supply of energy and almost all of the necessary nutrients, yet are natural, simple, and low in weight. Some of these foods will be mentioned later in this chapter. But even the most simplistic meals should be planned prior to leaving on a trip because, don't forget, for every day's worth of food you carry for going out into the woods, you must also pack a day's food for the return trip, plus food for the approximate number of days out.

CAMPING FOODS

Dried and Freeze-Dried Foods

Dried (dehydrated) foods are the best foods to take backpacking because they eliminate the weight of the water in the food. Dried foods are concentrated, containing the maximum amount of energy for their weight, and preserved to keep almost indefinitely under most conditions. You must, however, keep them dry. They are very easy to prepare, requiring little or no cooking. When you take dried foods, you're carrying a minimal amount of weight and a maximum number of calories. When you carry freeze-dried foods, you carry even less water with you. It makes no sense to try to carry whole, fresh foods. It's possible, but impractical because fresh foods weigh so much. For fresh foods, rely on wild foods. During the warmer months you will be able to pick your own fruits and vegetables, after a little practice. (See section on Foraging for wild foods.)

If you think you can't make it without your regular diet, you can now get everything you can imagine in freeze-dried form. Any variety of relatively simple, natural foods may be easily supplemented, expanded, or even replaced by selections from the enormous variety of prepackaged, dehydrated, and freeze-dried foods found in your nearest outdoor or outfitting store.

These foods are usually packaged in two-serving, four-serving, or larger, bulk packs in oxygen- and moisture-proof containers (foil pouches, for instance). All come complete with cooking instructions, and most are precooked, requiring only the addition of boiling water or very minimal cooking and a few minutes of resting time for complete water absorption and "food set-up."

You can eat anything from western or cheese omelettes, french toast, and blueberry pancakes to sausage and hash-brown potatoes for breakfast; and everything from pork chops, rib-eye steaks, ham-flavored soybean steaks (for vegetarians), beef stew, turkey tetrazzini, and chili, to lasagna for lunch or dinner. For dessert, you can have strawberries à la crème, pineapple cheesecake, or vanilla, chocolate, or strawberry ice cream. A complete line of vegetables and fruits is also available.

If you plan to take mostly freeze-dried meals, the best way to organize this extensive list of foods is to either go to the outfitting store or, better yet, get a catalog or two from companies that make the foods and look them over. From the catalogs' complete listings, you can decide what you'd like and, since the weights and prices are included, exactly how much weight you'll be carrying and how much the food will cost.

Although the advantages associated with these prepackaged freeze-dried and dehydrated foods are obvious, there are also a few disadvantages. It has been my experience that they are not always the delectable, tempting treats that are advertised on the packages. In fact, more than a few that I have tried have been terrible excuses for food. Most items are very expensive. Finally, meals that promise to feed two people are often barely sufficient for one, especially after a full day of hiking. I would suggest trying a dinner or two of different brands of freeze-dried food at home before buying out the camping store.

I always take a few freeze-dried dinners when I go backpacking, as insurance in case I want to stay out for several extra days. However, I prefer to take simple, natural foods when camping. It seems incongruous to eat lobster Newburg and chocolate ice cream in the middle of the Rockies. As long as you're leaving most of the excesses of civilization at home, why not leave the rich meals behind, too? After a week of hiking and eating simple foods, your body will feel clean and refreshed.

All of the foods I take may be purchased at your grocery store or local health-food store. I carry the following types of foods and mix them to create all of my meals. Suggested recipes using these ingredients are listed at the end of the chapter, but variations are endless and fun to concoct.

Grains

Grains are the basis for my hot breakfasts and dinners at the campsite. One and a half cups of dried whole grains should be plenty for a meal for two people, but check the amount for yourself at home. I take grains in three forms: whole, ground or rolled in cereal form, and finely ground in mixes for breads and pancakes.

Whole grains can be packed, cooked, and eaten as is—there's rice (I use brown rice), wheat, oats, corn, buckwheat, barley, millet, rye, and more. Eat grains for dinner when you're particularly hungry. To dress them up, add dried onion and parsley along with bouillon cubes or curry powder. Or make up a tomato soup mix, add oregano and basil, and pour it over rice. Make a stew with any wild foods you find. The biggest disadvantage of whole grains is that they can take as much as twenty-five minutes of boiling to prepare; so if you have time, soak them first to reduce cooking time. Easier yet, take most of your grains ground up in the form of cereals, which require very little cooking time.

I have a hand grain-grinder at home and grind my own; if you don't own a grain mill, be sure you get whole-grain ground cereals, which can be purchased at the local health-food store or at a good supermarket.

Most all the grains are good as cereal, but when I go backpacking I always grind up enough corn for several days or a week and take this along for morning cereal and pancakes. Why corn, other than it's my favorite? In talking about his experiences in the early 1900s among the Indians of the Southwest, Wharton James comments on the food value of this simple dried grain:

I had gone off with a band of Indians on a hard week's ride with no other food than parched corn and a few raisins. This was chewed and chewed by the hour, a handful making an excellent meal, and thoroughly nourishing the perfect bodies of these stalwart athletes, who never knew an ache or pain, and who could withstand fatigue and hardship without a thought.
(*Learning From the Indians*, Wharton James, p. 125)

I also take oatmeal (ground or rolled oats), rice, and wheat as cereals for breakfast, lunch, or dinner. To these I add dried fruit, cinnamon, powdered milk, and sweetening. Oatmeal with dried apples, cinnamon, and honey is particularly delicious, as is cornmeal with maple syrup. Any of these cereals, whether made from one grain or several, is especially delicious with wild fruits. It's a good idea to soak your cereals and dried fruit, too. Use the container from your mess kit and soak them together in water overnight. In the morning, simply put the pan on the fire, water and all. In this way the cooking time is cut by more than half, and you gain vitamins and minerals that are normally lost during longer cooking processes.

I take wheat along in a slightly different form. After grinding it to a very fine cereal—the consistency of coarse flour—I add either nonfat dry milk or Tiger's Milk (a protein supplement) at the rate of three eighths cup per each cup of wheat, a large pinch of sea salt, and baking powder at the rate of two teaspoons per each cup of flour. This serves as a ready-to-go mix for pancakes, biscuits, and cinnamon, herb, and pan breads. (See the recipes listed later in this chapter.) The same formula can be followed using any ground-grain flour or a mixture of any two or more of them, to make quick, delicious, and nourishing bread foods.

Nuts, Seeds, and Dried Fruits

Nuts, seeds, and dried fruits are all excellent camping foods because they are high in energy, vitamins, and minerals; keep well; weigh little; and may be eaten raw. They are the foods I eat on the trail and are the basis of my diet while backpacking. Available dried fruits include apricots, pears, cherries, peaches, prunes, apples, dates, figs, raisins, currants, and pineapple. Nuts available include almonds, cashews, peanuts, hazelnuts, and Brazil nuts. Seeds include sunflower, sesame, pumpkin, and chia. Nuts and seeds can also be carried in the "gerry tubes" (refillable polyurethane tubes with a screw cap and a plastic clip closure on the bottom) in the form of butter, such as peanut butter, cashew butter, or sesame butter. These lists are not complete by any means, so take your favorites.

Various, delicious, ready-to-eat combinations of these ingredients, such as granolas, trail mixes, and energy bars, may be easily prepared at home ahead of time.

Soups

I usually take lots of dried soups because they are lightweight, refreshing, nourishing, and very easy to fix. Just add hot or boiling water and, for added richness, some powdered milk. There are endless varieties at the grocery store—vegetable, meat, meat and vegetable, bean, pea, and so on. Take your favorites.

I have found that tomato soup tastes particularly good, and it also doubles, when you are hot and tired, as tomato juice (chill it in an ice-cold spring or river). I also take lots of bouillon cubes—vegetable, chicken, or beef. Hot or cold, they're instant energy and protein and weigh practically nothing.

Beverages

The best cold drink you'll find while backpacking is cool, clear, delicious water. For hot drinks, I suggest herb teas, regular tea, hot chocolate, or coffee. Blackstrap molasses with hot water makes a refreshing beverage. Take your favorites.

Sweetenings

I try to eat as little refined sugar as possible. So though it means carrying a little extra weight, I make this allowance and take either honey, blackstrap molasses, maple syrup, or jams or jellies homemade with honey.

Fat

You will need a little fat for frying, for greasing pans when making bread, and for keeping foods from drying out when broiling. I take some form of pure pressed soya or corn oil, which works, tastes good, and, if placed in a tube with a tight cap, is not a problem to carry.

Spices and Herbs

These are a treat in the woods. They seem to taste twice as good as at home and thus are a welcome addition to any cooked foods—breads, soups, beverages, and pancakes. They also weigh almost nothing, so you can take almost any variety you like. I carry powdered onion, oregano, celery salt, garlic, cinnamon, nutmeg, salt, and pepper and always substitute fresh wild herbs such as onion and garlic whenever possible. As I mentioned earlier, film containers are excellent for carrying spices.

Miscellaneous Extras

I always take a bag of powdered milk and a bag of powdered eggs for eating and adding to breads, desserts, and other dishes.

RECIPES

Ready-To-Eat Trail Foods

Christian's Crunchy Quickstart. This is my favorite simple food or trail ration and is very nutritious and easily prepared. I carry at least two handfuls for each day I will be out, though it's so good I usually end up eating more! I eat it for meals and for snacks. It's very high in protein and energy.

> Mix: (Add your favorites or delete according to your own tastes.)
> 4 cups rolled oats
> 1 cup wheat germ or bran
> 2 cups unsweetened shredded coconut
> ½ cup sesame seeds
> 1 cup sunflower seeds (hulled)
> ½ cup flax seeds

½ cup rye, wheat, or soy flakes
1 cup soybeans, roasted, whole or halved
1 cup chopped nuts (Almonds and cashews are good.)
1 cup nonfat dry milk
Heat: (Do not boil!)
½ cup safflower or soya oil
¼ cup blackstrap molasses (or more to your taste)
¾ cup honey
¾ cup sesame or peanut butter (I like sesame.)
½ tsp. vanilla extract
½ tsp. salt

Stir the liquid into the dry ingredients, coating them thoroughly. Bake in small batches on a cookie sheet or a shallow baking pan at 350° until light, golden brown, *turning frequently because it burns very easily!*

Let cool and add:
1 cup raisins or currants, or both
1 cup chopped figs, dates, sun-dried apricots, or your favorite dried fruit.

J's Trail Mix. Here's another good recipe that requires no preliminary cooking. Again, add your favorite or delete according to your own tastes.

2 pounds figs or dates (Black mission figs are my favorite.)
½ cup sesame seeds

Quarter the figs or dates or cut smaller if you like. Then roll the pieces in the sesame seeds, coating them well.

Add:
1 cup sunflower seeds (hulled)
1 cup nuts (Almonds are my favorite.)
1 cup raisins
1 cup other dried fruit (Apples or apricots are my favorite.)

Stir or mix well and bag up for the trip.

Energy Bars. When I have time, I prefer to make energy bars for myself. Here's the basic recipe, of which I've made countless variations.

Mix:

½ cup peanut butter

½ cup sesame butter

⅔ cup sunflower seeds (whole or ground)

3–4 tbsp. honey

¼ cup raisins

¼ cup dates or figs, finely chopped

¼ cup chia seeds

½ cup nuts (almonds, cashews, peanuts, etc.), finely chopped
or ground

Stir in:

1 tbsp. brewer's yeast or soy flour

½–⅔ cup powdered milk

Shape into small rectangular bars. Roll in shredded coconut. Chill in refrigerator or let sit overnight in a cool place. Wrap individually for the trail.

Suggestions: You want the final product to be very firm, so if it's too gooey, add more powdered milk. This is just one recipe, of which there are countless variations. If you like, experiment and make your own energy bars ahead of time. In health-food stores you can buy good energy bars containing everything from dates to bee pollen. However, if you have time, it's fun to make your own.

Pancakes and Breads

All-purpose Mix

Grind wheat to a very fine cereal—the consistency of coarse flour.

Add:

Nonfat dry milk or Tiger's Milk (a protein supplement) at
the rate of ⅜ cup for each cup of wheat flour

Large pinch of sea salt

Baking powder at the rate of 2 tsps. for each cup of wheat
flour

This mixture is the basis for the following recipes. The same formula can be followed using any ground-grain flour or a mixture of any two or more of them.

Pancakes (Wheatcakes, Corncakes, etc.).
Mix:
    1 or 2 cups All-purpose Mix
    1 tbsp. dried powdered eggs (These are optional and are for
        added richness and flavor, so if you don't have
        any extra along, it's OK.)
    1 tbsp. sweetening
Stir in:
    Enough water to make a batter the consistency of melted
        ice cream
Grease your mess kit frying pan and cook.

My *favorite variations:* To the batter, add wild berries, cinnamon, nutmeg, nuts, or anything else you like and serve with pure maple syrup, honey, jams, or jellies or with crushed wild berries on top. Cinnamon-nut-berry pancakes are my absolute favorite.

Pan Bread. The Indians called this "bannock," and it's especially good when made with corn flour.
Mix:
    1 or 2 cups All-purpose Mix
    1 tbsp. fat
Add:
    Enough warm water to make a soft dough
Lightly grease any pan in the mess kit. Flatten dough so that it's approximately ½ inch thick in the pan. Cook over coals 5–10 minutes, lightly browning both sides. Baking may also be done Indian style. They cooked on a large flat rock, held in the air by three or four small ones, under which they built a fire. They used the slow, steady heat of the stone to bake the bread on both sides. In fact, I think this method is superior to baking in a pan and can be used to cook foods other than bread.

My *favorite variations:* If you want sweet bread, add sweetening, cinnamon, wild berries, or dried fruit. For spice or herb bread, add wild or dried onions, celery salt, oregano, and sage. For nut bread, add any kind of nuts with sweetening and chopped figs and/or dates.

Stickbread

Mix:
   1 or 2 cups All-purpose Mix
   1 tbsp. dried powdered eggs (optional)
   1 tbsp. sweetening
   1 tbsp. fat
Add:
   Enough water to make a soft dough

Roll the dough into individual round strips – 1 foot long and ½–¾ inch wide. Wrap each strip in a spiral around one end of a greased stick. (Be sure to leave enough room between coils for the dough to expand.) Push the other end of the stick (sharpened) into the ground near the fire to bake. Turn to bake both sides.

My favorite variations: This is delicious with cinnamon and honey.

Dirtbread. There is one other method for making good bread – by the loaf. Simply move the coals and ashes of your campfire aside, put the dough on the ground where they were, and cover the dough with *grayish* ashes – not too many live coals. Bake, dust off when finished, and eat. I've done this many times, and, surprisingly enough, the bread bakes fairly uniformly and comes out done and beautifully browned – if your fire's not too hot.

Desserts

Desserts are a special treat; with the same ingredients I discussed in the Grains section, you can make great desserts with a little ingenuity.

Rice Pudding

Cook:
   1 cup whole brown rice (or 2 cups ground)
   1 pinch of salt if not using the All-purpose Mix
Add:
   1 tbsp. powdered eggs
   1 handful raisins (or any other dried or fresh wild fruit)
   1 small handful nuts (or granola or trail mix)

½ cup powdered milk if not using the All-purpose Mix
1 large pinch cinnamon
Sweetening to taste

Reheat and serve.

Pies and Cobblers

Mix:
1 cup All-purpose Mix
1 tbsp. fat
Add:
Enough cold water to make a pie dough

Soak dried fruit in water or collect wild fruit. Spread the dough evenly in the low-edged pan of your mess kit. Then fill the shell with the hydrated dried fruit. Apples, apricots, peaches, or prunes are all good. Better yet, fill with any fresh wild fruits you have found, such as cherries, blueberries, blackberries, raspberries, or grapes. Prepare fresh berries by crushing them and removing some of the juice. Top the fruit with sweetening, cinnamon, and nutmeg and bake near the fire on a rock or on old coals for approximately ½–¾ hour, or until done.

Quickstart Cookies

Mix:
1 cup All-purpose Mix
1 tbsp. powdered eggs
2 large handfuls Quickstart
1 pinch cinnamon (optional)
1 tbsp. honey or other sweetening (more if desired)
Add:
Enough water to make a stiff cookie dough

Stir in the water and mix well. Form into cookies. Grease the bottom of your pan and "oven-pan-bake" until golden brown. (Use the frying pan as the bottom and the deep dish or cereal pan—this one forms the other side of the assembled mess kit—as the top.)

This, then, is the way I eat when I go backpacking. Dried fruits, nuts, seeds, my Quickstart, J's Trail Mix, grains, cereals, bread mixes, dried soups, beverages, herbs and spices, energy rations, and a few extras (freeze-dried foods) make up the food in my pack.

4. On the Trail

WHEN AND HOW TO HIKE

Hiking is much easier and much more enjoyable in the early morning when it's cooler and when you're more rested and have lots of energy. I usually get up with the sun and complete my ten or fifteen miles for the day by lunchtime. This leaves the afternoon free for exploring, fishing, foraging for wild foods, or just lying in the sun.

Your hiking speed will vary depending on the terrain and your physical condition. Don't tire yourself out trying to break speed records. I try to settle into a comfortable, medium-speed natural glide (from the hips), somewhere between the slow pace that rapidly tires me and a fast walk. Start out slowly, and you will find your own stride.

When hiking, pull your abdomen in, raise your chest, keep your chin down, and let your arms hang easily and naturally by your side. Place your feet softly on the ground with your toes pointing straight ahead and *glide* with a smooth, natural movement. Remember, always breathe with your mouth *closed*. Breathing through your nose filters out air impurities and replenishes the water vapor in your air passages.

When you carry your pack, lean forward slightly from the hips, and make each stride as long as you comfortably can. The pack should be a part of you and move with you, not against you. Push off to the next stride with your toes.

Rest when you become fatigued, but, if you're going to keep hiking, don't rest too long if you're not in top shape. Five or ten minutes should be sufficient—any longer and you're going to stiffen up. Get off your feet, lie or sit down, raise your feet, and relax fully. Have a small drink of water and/or an energy snack. I drink only when I rest and very sparingly then, because I only get thirstier if I drink while hiking. To keep my mouth moist I suck on a prune or date pit or on a smooth stone that is large enough that I won't swallow it.

HOW TO ADJUST YOUR PACK

This is very important and will take some experimenting the first day out. If your pack is not adjusted properly, you will be very uncomfortable and will become exhausted quickly. Experts say about 75 percent of the pack's weight is supposed to be transferred from the shoulder area to the legs and hips through the waist belt. The shoulder straps should carry approximately one quarter of the pack's weight, thus acting primarily as pack guides. They should be tight enough to ensure that pack and body move together, but not so tight as to restrict your movement, and not so loose as to allow too much free-pack movement.

Hoist the pack up a bit and pull the waist belt tight enough to allow this weight transfer. If the pack pulls back against your chest when you are walking uphill so that you have to lean forward to compensate, your shoulder straps are too loose. After a day or so of hiking you will get a feel for just how to carry your pack and be able to adjust it in seconds. However, the first day out, keep adjusting it until it is comfortable.

ORIENTATION

Maps and Map Reading

As I mentioned before, the best maps are topographics. Once you have a good map, make sure that you learn how to read it and can put its information to use.

Most of the map signs, symbols, and configurations are self-explanatory. In general, anything that is man-made, such as a highway, road, building, railroad, town, or bridge, is marked in RED or BLACK. A hiking trail is designated by a single, *very* small dotted black line. These are sometimes difficult to distinguish, so look closely.

Any marking in BLUE means some form of water. Lakes, streams (thin lines), rivers (thick lines), and swamps are all shown in blue. An intermittent stream or river is designated by a dotted blue line. This stream may be a dry bed during the summer and a raging, icy torrent during spring break-up when the ice and snow melt in the higher altitudes. A stream may also vary greatly in volume over the course of *one day* during the spring. The same stream that is ankle deep in the morning may be up to your waist after the afternoon sun has melted the snow up in the hills.

BROWN lines are called "lines of contour," and they let you know where the hills, mountains, and valleys are located. The difference in elevation between individual lines is usually ten or twenty feet, but check the information given at the bottom of the map. The steeper the grade, the closer the brown contour lines are to one another. Every five or ten lines there is a line marked with its altitude. The elevations of mountain peaks are also labeled.

GREEN, of course, designates forest areas. Check the date that your map was published. If it was fifteen, twenty, or thirty years ago, don't be surprised to find substantial changes in the terrain. In twenty years a field may become a young forest or an old forest may be chopped or burned down. This is also more than sufficient time for streams and rivers to substantially change course, so don't be surprised if they don't appear to be exactly as mapped, either. In these cases, rely on the lines of contour to figure out your exact location on the map.

Simple Navigation

The knack of being able to look at the map, look at the land, and say with some degree of confidence that you are here and that is so-and-so mountain takes a little more finesse and practice than simply reading the map. This orientation process is greatly aided by a compass. Now that you have made yourself familiar with a topographic

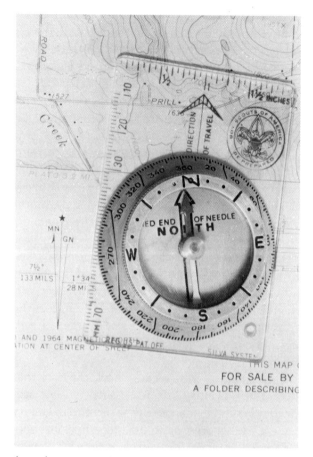

A good compass and a topographical map are essential for orienting yourself in unfamiliar territory. Photo by Emil Ghinger.

map and can relate to its mountains, valleys, plateaus, woods, swamps, lakes, and streams, you can begin to think about the compass and its relation to you and the map.

Basically there are two types of compasses. The simple type—needle or dial—has only a scale plus the needle or dial. The more sophisticated types of compasses have movable cases or housings and a north-south orienting arrow. Either type is perfectly adequate.

You can tell time with a compass and a matchstick. East is
approximately 3:00 P.M.

Orienting the Map

The map is not much good to you unless you know which direction you are facing. First, you need to "orient" both yourself and the
terrain to the map using the compass. This is simple: Spread the map
out on a flat surface on the ground and place the compass on it, allowing the needle to settle at north. Locate the north-south lines on the
map. These are the two little arrows located on the bottom of the map.
The arrow labeled MN indicates magnetic north, and the arrow labeled

GN indicates geographic north. You want magnetic north; geographic north will be explained later.

If you have a simple needle compass, simply turn the map, holding the compass so that the needle stays at north, until the magnetic north arrow on the map becomes parallel with the compass needle. Now you have the north of your map exactly coinciding with the north of your compass.

If you have a more sophisticated compass, turn the case or housing until the north-marker orienting arrow is parallel to and pointing north with the magnetic needle. Now turn the map, holding the compass fast, until the magnetic-north arrow on the map agrees with the magnetic compass needle.

In either case, the map and you are now oriented. All directions on the map agree with those of your surroundings. You are now ready to travel, but first position yourself so that you're able to get a clear view of things. Look around in all the different directions and try to identify mountain peaks, rivers, swamps, buildings, and other similar, obvious landmarks and to locate the landmarks on the map.

Laying a Course

The next step is to "lay a course." This is the one other simple operation you should be able to perform to navigate using your compass. Laying a course and other useful tips are usually explained fully and clearly in the instructions that come with your compass. However, for those who have long since lost those instructions and for those who have resurrected old army or Boy Scout compasses, here goes. First, a little background is necessary.

There are four cardinal compass directions—North, South, East, and West, and four general in-between directions—Northeast, Southeast, Southwest, and Northwest. The compass is marked with the 360 degrees of the circle; the degrees are used to designate the different directions. North is at 000°, East at 090°, South at 180°, and West at 270°. It is a good idea to speak of compass directions using three digits to avoid mistakes and confusion.

The simplest use of the compass is taking a reading from you to an object or landmark that is stationary. This is easy. If you have a simple needle compass, turn yourself squarely toward the landmark. Next,

Sighting the compass to a landmark. Photo by Emil Ghinger.

turn the compass until the needle lines up with the north marking. Now sight to the landmark, across the compass, and read the heading from the side of the compass nearest the landmark.

If you have a more sophisticated type of compass (again, with a movable housing and north-marker orienting arrow), point the directional arrow squarely at the landmark, and then turn the movable case or top until the north-marker orienting arrow lies under the floating magnetic-north needle – at north. Now simply read the heading to the landmark at the directional arrow.

Before using the map to lay a course you will need a little more background. Compass needles point to magnetic north. Remember back a few paragraphs when I mentioned that there is a configuration indicating north on the bottom of topographic maps? Well, one arrow is magnetic north, which is indicated by the compass needle, and the other arrow indicates the true geographic (map) north, where the North Pole is located. Near the little arc in between the two arrows you will find a number. This number of degrees is called the compass variation or declination—for the particular area on that map. The number of degrees varies according to your relative position, east or west of an imaginary line marked 000° declination. In our hemisphere this line runs from the North Pole south through Lake Michigan to just east of Florida, then down through the Caribbean Sea into western Venezuela and on south. If you are located *west* of 000° declination, your compass will point a little to the east of true north (geographic north). If you are located *east* of 000° declination, it will point a little to the west of true geographic north. The number of degrees that the compass will point to the west or east of true north is already given to you on the topographic map or on other good maps for the areas that they cover. The reason for this adjustment is that the "magnetic North Pole," to which the compass needle is attracted, is actually located some 1,400 miles to the south of the true North Pole.

Your map shows true geographic north, not magnetic north. Thus, to get true readings with your compass and to walk in the right direction, you must, after you take the compass reading, correct for the number of degrees "off" your compass points from true geographic north. If this correction is less than 10°, I tend to ignore it. However, it can be substantial in areas that are located far away from 000° declination. These areas include the northern Atlantic and Pacific coasts of the United States, eastern and western Canada, and Alaska.

When working from the map to terrain, the rule is: *West is Best*—add westerly declination or variation to your compass readings—and *East is Least*—subtract easterly declination or variation from the compass readings *before* traveling. For example, suppose you're hiking in Olympic National Park in Washington and you want to walk to a point that the map says is directly east (090°) of you. In Olympic National Park, the declination is approximately 024° East. So to arrive at your destination, you would have to follow a heading of 090° *minus 024° or 066°* on your compass. Now suppose you're in the same situation in Baxter State Park in Maine. Here the declination or variation is approximately 20° West. So you would follow a heading of *090° plus 020° or 110°* on your compass to go east to the river.

If you know where you are on the map and where you want to go, for example, an old mine or a mountain, you can now use the compass to give you a fairly accurate heading or bearing to reach your intended destination.

If you have a simple needle compass, orient the map and place the center of the compass over your position on the oriented map. If you don't know exactly where you are, you can easily approximate your position by sighting several landmarks that you believe to be those marked on the map and figuring out your position relative to the landmarks. Now read the compass along a direct line from its center to your destination. Make the necessary correction for variation (declination) and proceed. If you want to make the declination correction before you take the reading, simply rotate the map and the compass *together* until the needle moves the amount of declination (the number of degrees from north) for that area. Then take the reading and proceed.

If you have the other type of compass, one with a movable housing, orient the map, placing the straight edge of the compass on the map, so that it connects the place where you are located with your intended destination. Turn the movable housing until the north-marker orienting arrow points to north on the map. Now, with the directional arrow pointing away from you, turn the whole compass until the magnetic needle lines up with the north-marker orienting arrow. After making the correction for declination, follow the heading of the directional arrow. After a few times, this whole process becomes reflex.

Regardless of the type of compass you have, if you want to eliminate the need for variation or declination correction, you can draw the magnetic north-south lines on the map ahead of time and simply use these lines as the map's true north-south lines.

TRAVEL, WITH AND WITHOUT A COMPASS

When I'm starting to hike in an area that is new to me, I take a quick look at my surroundings; I also take a compass reading. Along the way I take several more readings to re-establish my general direction of travel.

I also make it a point, following the example of the Indians, to notice where the sun is in relation to my hiking direction, that is, where the sun strikes me when I'm facing in the direction I want to travel. It is helpful to know that the sun rises in the east, sets in the west, and arcs higher in the summer than in the winter. The travel path of the sun in the northern hemisphere during the winter is noticeably south of its zenith (the point in the sky that is directly overhead) and passes almost through the zenith during the summer. At noon in summer, the sun will be almost directly overhead, and at noon in winter it will be due south of you. If you're hiking in the southern hemisphere, it's exactly the opposite.

With a little practice you can fairly easily estimate directions and the time of day. If you get into the habit of taking a few compass readings and of frequently relating the sun's position to your direction of travel, you can easily retrace your steps if you become lost. For example, if I hiked in the early afternoon with the sun behind my left shoulder, I could easily hike toward my starting point later in the day by facing the sun (with correction for its movement throughout the afternoon) and keeping it on my right shoulder. Or, if I've been hiking generally 090°, or east, I can easily retrace my steps by heading back on 270°, or west.

These two simple navigational methods, plus a map and a sense of dead reckoning, have helped me find my way in and out of the woods many times. They have been especially important when I have ventured off the marked trails.

Dead Reckoning

This process is neither mystical nor complicated. It was practiced by the Indians long before the white man came to America. Dead reckoning is used when you know the general direction in which you want to go, but the trip will take you through the woods or over the plains or rugged terrain, and you are too far away from your destination to see it. Dead reckoning simply means finding your way by using landmarks. To do this, find an object or landmark in your path of travel — pick one that is distant but also clearly visible — and hike to it. When you get there or get almost there, pick another distant landmark and repeat this routine until you arrive at your destination.

If you need to go through a dense forest along the route, line up three trees. As you arrive at the first tree, line up another one beyond the remaining two; repeat this process until you pass through the woods. This method will keep you from walking in circles, which seems to be a natural tendency in the woods.

I always travel by dead reckoning when I leave regular hiking trails. Hiking by this method will improve your skills of observation. You will begin to notice objects in your surroundings and to remember them if you see them again when you're coming from another direction. Another helpful habit to start developing is looking back occasionally to establish the relative positions of various landmarks, such as hills, valleys, and stands of trees. A turn in a river, a huge old oak tree, and a strange rock formation can all look very different when seen from a different direction.

Other Travel Hints

If you don't have a compass, but have a watch with approximately the correct time for the local area, you can still determine directions. Point the hour hand directly toward the sun. Due south lies halfway between the hour hand and the 12. If the sun's not out, use a small straight stick held upright in the center of the watch so that its shadow falls along the hour hand. South will lie halfway between the shadow and the 12.

If you don't have a watch but do have a compass, it is possible to determine the approximate time. Place the compass on a flat surface and turn the compass so that the north marking lines up with the needle. Now take a small straight stick (a match will do) and place it upright directly in the center of the compass. The shadow cast by the stick will tell you what time it is.

Of course it is not really necessary to use your compass to make a good guess at the time. Since you know that the sun is approximately (as I mentioned before, its position varies slightly with the season) south at 12 noon; east at 6 a.m.; and west at 6 p.m. This means that the sun is approximately in the southeast at 9 a.m., and in the southwest at 3 p.m.

At night, it is also possible to find your way by using the *stars*. If you can find the Big Dipper, use the two end stars of the bowl of the dipper as pointers to find the North Star, or Pole Star, which is the end star in the handle of the Little Dipper. *True north always* lies at the horizon directly under the North, or Pole, Star because this star always stays in the same place while the other stars seem to move in circles across the sky.

Now, if you want to practice "finding your way," a good test of your abilities is the old "crow fly hike." Go directly from one point to another, over and through all obstacles—woods, rivers, valleys—compensating for all detours, and return via another route.

CHOOSING A CAMPSITE

When

Plan your day so that you are camped, feeling good and comfortable, and moving slowly and easily with the pace of the woodlands before sundown. Pitch your tent, get your fire ready, and secure your pack while you still have plenty of light. Trying to set up camp and get organized for a comfortable night's rest in the dark is difficult and leads to breaking or losing equipment. Besides, you won't have any time to explore or to watch animals feed if you're hassling and hurrying with your tent at their feeding time, the hour just before and the hour just after sundown. It's also during this time that you make friends with your new home and develop a feeling for the spot that you have picked. You might want to consider stopping there again sometime, especially if moose, elk, or beaver feed close by.

How

The two most important criteria for selecting a campsite are nearby sources of good drinking water and dead, dry wood for fuel. An ideal spot would be a clearing on a gently sloping rise above a river on the

A campsite located one-third to one-half of the way up a rise. Photo by Emil Ghinger.

southeast side of a mature forest or woods. You'd have plenty of fire-wood, water, and protection from the north and west winds. A spot like this, however, is hard to find and nearly always some desired feature must be sacrificed.

Avoid camping directly in the lowest areas, especially if there's a body of water at the lowest point. If it's available, pick a spot slightly above a river or lake, that is, a third to half of the way up a rise. These spots will be warmer and dryer at night, much cooler during the day, and, most importantly, *much less buggy*. In low-lying land you will find marshes, swamps, and wet areas, which are breeding grounds for mosquitoes and "no-see-'ums"—tiny, pin-head size insects that are 100 percent teeth and jaws!—and faster streams, which are breeding grounds for black flies. If you camp too near these areas you will regret it.

A "V" drainage ditch around the tent can cause soil erosion.
Photo by Emil Ghinger.

Pure Luxury

If it's possible, try to find a slight slope rising to the west and open to the east. Why? Because it is very pleasurable to be gently wakened by the rising sun shining into your tent, and the gentle slope helps the water run off if it rains heavily. Do *not* dig a "V" drainage ditch around your tent; you're just going to cause ground erosion. Your treated tent floor, which extends up the sides of the tent, will be enough protection.

A little tree shade is always nice, but be careful to check the health of your shade trees. Don't camp under any that are dead or that may fall into your camp. Also avoid stands of poplars or conifers because these trees have widespreading, shallow root systems and fall easily. Remember, too, that after a rain too many dripping branches will keep your sleeping area and tent damp for hours.

Finally, try to find the most beautiful spot you can, within these limits. When you think you've found a spot to your liking, sit down, take a good look around, and think about it for a while before pitching your tent and stowing your gear. Enjoy.

A Word About Water

Be very careful about the water you drink on a camping trip. Water is one of the best mediums for carrying viruses and bacteria and is probably responsible for some 95 percent of all stomach-related gastrointestinal problems that people get while traveling. If you're in a real wilderness area, miles from any permanent human habitation, chances are that both the ground and surface waters are pure and safe. Ground water includes spring water from rock or ground openings, and any water emanating directly from the water table. Surface water is water running on the surface of the earth, such as rivers, and is much more likely to be contaminated.

If you're anywhere near the limits of permanent human habitation, the chances are that the surface water and sometimes part of the ground water are polluted. Rainwater and water from a spring's source are probably pure. It is important that you *not* consider spring water to be pure if you are not at the source, as there could be a pollutant, such as a dead animal, between you and that source.

Unless you're in a remote wilderness area or high enough in the mountains to be sure that no one lives above you, it's a good idea to purify surface water by boiling it for a minimum of five minutes. If for any reason you can't boil the water, you can purify it in half an hour by treating it with water purification tablets. There are two different types of water purification tablets, halazone and iodine. Halazone is sufficient except in tropical and subtropical areas; two tablets will purify a quart of water. Follow the directions on the bottle very closely; a good case of diarrhea and vomiting is not fun, especially if it could have been easily avoided. But remember, *boiling is best.*

SETTING UP YOUR CAMP

Pitching Your Tent

I usually break camp early in the morning when things are still a little wet from dew or rain, so the first thing I do on arriving at my next campsite is to pitch my tent, so that it has a chance to air and dry out.

Try to find a relatively open spot within a large natural wind-shelter to pitch your tent. Look the ground over carefully where you are about to set up the tent. A good sleeping surface should allow you to relax completely and should insulate you from the chill of the colder ground. It should be dry, smooth, soft, and insect-free. However, ground that is level and hard is much more comfortable than soft, uneven ground. Sleep level or on a slight slope. You'll slide and roll all night if the slope is too steep.

Clear the area of rocks, stones, and branches since these are very uncomfortable if left in place. Take special care to remove all sharp rocks and jagged pieces of wood. Even the strongest of tent floors can be cut or torn by these. After clearing the area, you can add to the comfort of your bed by placing already fallen or dead pine-bough ends or bunches of pine needles on the ground where the tent will be pitched.

The actual pitching method varies with the type of tent, but most rectangular-shaped backpacking tents I have seen roughly follow this pattern: Unroll the tent and place it on the ground, spreading the floor to its capacity, making sure that the end where you want your head is level with, or higher than, the foot end. I like to sleep with my head toward the entrance so that I can see the stars and the sunrise. Secure the tent floor all around by putting the tent pegs through the loops and driving them into the ground at a 30°–45° angle to the ground away from the tent. Driving the pegs in at an angle will prevent them from working themselves loose. Use your hands to drive in the pegs; if the ground is hard, use a rock. Then assemble and install the support poles and secure the front and back pole mainstays. Both poles, and consequently both ends of the tent, should be *vertical*. Secure the rest of the peg loops on the tent and the tent fly. Sometimes it is convenient to tie some of the tent lines to trees rather than to stakes in the ground.

When you are finished, there should be a wide air space between the rain fly and the tent walls. All lines should be taut, but not over-

Tent pegs should be placed at a 30° to 45° angle to the ground. Photo by Emil Ghinger.

stretched, so that the tent assumes and maintains its intended, full form. In the morning you might find that the lines need retightening, especially in damp areas or during wet weather.

On some backpacking tents, the tent-fly lines attach to the main tent-cord lines rather than to their own ground pegs. If this is the case with your tent, it is a good idea to tie the tent-fly lines to the main cords with a knot called a bowline. This makes a tight loop that is easily tied and untied and that will not slip under strain. Bowlines ensure that the tent fly will not droop and slowly collapse onto the tent, allowing condensation to form and moisture to permeate the inside tent walls.

If you are camping in very windy conditions or you think the possibility of a "blow" exists, you can simply and easily secure the tent by placing medium-sized rocks (six to eight inches in diameter) on all the tent and tent-fly pegs and/or in the inside four corners of the tent. Inside the tent, try to use the smooth round variety to avoid tearing the fabric. This practice is always a good idea if you are pitching your tent on sandy soil, such as a beach, instead of on a harder surface. To do

Note the wide air space between the rain fly and the tent walls. Photo by Emil Ghinger.

this, you obviously have to drive the tent pegs in until the tops are almost level with the ground, but this will secure the tent, providing it's pitched properly, in all but a tornado. (If a tornado hits, the tent won't help anyway.)

After The Tent's Up

If the weather is particularly bad and you are concerned about being a little cold, remember that insulation from the ground is more important than an extra cover. Spread your rain poncho over the tent floor and put the ground mat and sleeping bag on top of it. A down vest makes an excellent warm pillow. If your socks are damp (not soaking wet!), pull them into your bag; they'll be warm and dry in the morning.

If you're hiking in very cold weather, you can do what many North American Indians did while traveling. Take coals from the fire and warm a spot of earth for several hours. Then scrape the coals away and cover the spot with leaves, pine needles, or more earth and pitch the tent or just throw your mat and bag on the ground that has been thoroughly warmed.

Now that your tent is set up and your ground mat and sleeping bag are in place, you will want to stow the rest of your gear. Don't leave equipment scattered here and there, or you will end up with a series of booby traps. Every object should have a designated spot and should be there when it is not in use. Since you are carrying a bare minimum of equipment to keep down the weight you have to tote, you don't want to lose or break anything through carelessness. After dark the advantage of an orderly campsite quickly becomes evident. You don't want to stumble over your boots, stab yourself with your knife, or strangle yourself on a clothesline. In fact, while you still have light, take a good look at the position of your tent lines so that you don't trip over them during the night.

Keep your boots in the corner of your tent overnight. This protects them from dew and rain. However, *never* keep your pack in the tent if you're in bear country. A bear may smell the food in the pack and come into your tent after it.

I keep my pack with my food in one of two places, depending on where I'm camping. If I'm in a remote area that is not regularly used by other backpackers, I stand my pack against a tree at least ten yards away from my tent. I usually spread my rain poncho on the tent floor; if I'm not using it there, I wrap it around the pack as extra protection against small animals and rain.

If you're camping in an area that gets heavy use, especially if it is near a garbage barrel or dump or has bits of trash strewn around, you should take extra precautions. Locate two small saplings that are about ten to twelve feet apart at a good distance from your tent. Choose trees that have trunks with small diameters—about six inches is good—and have side branches at about the same level. Lodge a pole horizontally from one sapling to the other, using the branches as supports. The pole should be at least twelve feet above the ground. Now throw your extra rope over the horizontal pole, tie the pack to one end, hoist the pack

Suspending your pack on a pole lodged between two saplings will keep it out of the way of hungry bears. Photo by Emil Ghinger.

up in the air out of "bear reach," and tie the other end to a tree. I suspend my whole pack, not just my food, because bears who hang around picnic areas or much-used campgrounds are hip to backpacks and will rip them apart to check for a meal. I strongly recommend using this method in heavily camped areas in bear territory, especially if you know that there is a bear who visits the site regularly (check for claw marks on the trees and obvious signs of human habitation, such as garbage). Bears can easily demolish food containers that are left on the ground and can climb trees with thick trunks to get at packs hung from branches. Bears are ingenious thieves and should be treated with respect.

BUILDING A FIRE

Selecting a Site

Be very careful when selecting a site to build your fire. Don't choose a spot that is very windy or that will give your fire a chance to spread. Better to eat cold, raw food or not to eat at all for a night than start a forest fire!

The site should be ten feet away from all trees, overhanging branches, and anything else that can catch fire—your tent, for example. Always build a fire on bare mineral soil, by which I mean a sandy, rocky, or gravel surface. Fires built on humus or soft earth surfaces eventually result in scarring and ground erosion. Therefore, to disrupt our vanishing wilderness as little as possible, please remember to build your fire on mineral soil. You can use one large flat stone or place several small flat stones together for a rocky base. If you're camping by a river or stream, build the fire on the sandy shore. If you have the choice, build on dry rather than wet ground. Clear an area on the ground approximately ten feet in diameter around the spot on which you are going to build the fire. It must be completely free of all inflammable material. This gives you a margin of safety against wind-blown sparks.

If a designated area with a fire receptacle is available, build your fire in it. If you come across another campfire site that has been used by someone before you, use it rather than constructing another one. There are many campsites that have been ruined by too many people building campfires. If you can't find a rocky, sandy, or gravel surface and there is no fire receptacle, *don't build* a campfire. Use your backpacking stove, if you have one. If you are in an emergency situation and must build on a humus surface, clear the area and carefully dig a small pit down to gravel or hardpan and build your fire in the depression. When you are through, refill the pit.

Gathering Materials

After you have selected and cleared the site, gather your materials. Gather all of them before you strike the match so that the fire won't keep going out for lack of fuel while you are trying to start it and so that you won't have to leave the fire once it's going. In fact, **never** leave a fire unattended; stick close by it!

You'll need tinder or kindling (the smallest and most flammable material), pencil- or finger-sized wood, and wrist- and log-sized wood. The best tinder I've found are the tiny, brittle, dead dry twigs from the trunks of evergreens. Evergreens are softwoods, which ignite and burn faster than hardwoods, and so are better for starting fires. You can also use dry leaves, dry grass, pine cones, or dry bark from a dead tree as kindling. The outer bark of a dead birch tree burns particularly well. Look for curls of birch bark lying around a living yellow birch tree.

Always use dead wood for the firewood. Never cut a live tree for a fire; green wood doesn't burn, anyway. The best fires are made with standing dead wood, that is, dead branches that are still on the tree, or a whole dead tree that has not yet fallen. This wood does not readily absorb rain or other moisture, unlike wood that is lying on the damp forest floor. The dead, dry, standing branches were the choice of Indian women for their cooking fires and were thus called "squaw wood." If you do use wood from a dead tree that is lying on the ground, select the branches that are not touching the ground. It's a good bet that the branches lying on the ground are wet clear through.

Firewood should be dry or seasoned and ready to burn. You can easily tell whether or not wood is dead and ready for burning: Most dead branches are brittle and will readily snap when broken; live ones bend. Wood that has been split will burn much more readily than whole logs. To get your fire going, you can split some of the smaller pieces of wood with two rocks (one as splitter, blunt and round, and the other as wedge, thinner and sharp), your hunting knife, or a hatchet if you carry one.

Types of Wood

The type and availability of firewood will vary depending on where you travel. In most cases, you'll probably have to use whatever is at hand, but when there is some choice, you will quickly find that all woods do not burn equally well. Some burn very quickly with a lot of heat and produce short-lived coals; some take longer to ignite, burn more slowly, and produce lasting, hot coals; and some don't burn very well at all.

In general, the hardwoods, such as oak, hickory, maple, ash, locust, ironwood (hornbeam), beech, and birch make nice, even, slow-burning fires with lots of heat and long-lasting hot coals. So if hardwoods

88

are available, choose them for your cooking fire. Softwoods usually burn more quickly, producing a very hot fire, but without long-lasting coals. Softwoods include pine, fir, spruce, linden (basswood), and the poplars (cottonwood and aspen). Softwoods are much better for starting than for maintaining fires. However, since they are much easier to ignite and burn faster than hardwoods, they are ideal for a quick fire to boil water or make soup. If you can find dead wood from a wild apple, pear, or cherry tree, you will have a special treat because these woods smell wonderful as they burn.

The greatest variety of trees and firewood in North America is found in the eastern broadleaf and coniferous forests. These forests run from the Atlantic Ocean to a line just west of the Great Lakes and the Mississippi River and from the southern United States to southern Canada. Here you'll find both hardwoods and softwoods in great variety. The choices for firewood in the western regions of the United States, in Alaska, and in western and northern Canada are going to be fewer. Here the forests are primarily coniferous, which means a lot of softwoods —pine, fir, spruce, cedar, and other evergreens—but the hardwoods are going to be almost nonexistent.

However, almost any dry wood (again, the best kind is standing dead wood) with perhaps one exception will provide a satisfactory fire for cooking. The exception is hemlock, an evergreen, that can be easily identified by its small, blunt needles arranged in graceful sprays on sweeping branches and by tiny upside-down needles on the underside of its twigs. This wood is known as the "fireworks firewood" because of its high resin content. Although it will produce a cooking fire, it may also provide charred clothing and flesh or a forest fire in the process.

Making Your Fire

After you have chosen and cleared your fire space and have gathered your materials, build the fire. Begin by assembling a simple fireplace. If there is not too much wind, you can lay the fireplace on the surface of the ground. Use stones or logs, whichever is available. If you are using rocks, collect enough to make a ring around an area the size of your intended fire. Choose rocks that are about the same size and are more or less flat on the top and bottom. If your fire doesn't get enough

Note the two logs on either side of the fire. A well-constructed cooking crane can hold up to a 3-gallon pail. Photo by Emil Ghinger.

air, make an air space on the windward side by moving a rock to leave a small gap.

Alternately, you can build your fireplace of logs. Find two logs that are about two to four feet long and four to eight inches in diameter. Place them on either side of your intended fire site, parallel to the direction of the wind, positioning them close enough together so that your cooking pots can sit right on the logs. Lay the fire between the logs. The logs will eventually catch and become a part of the fire. If you're

Pull the partially burned logs out of the fire before going to sleep. Photo by Emil Ghinger.

having trouble getting the fire started because of too much wind, place the logs perpendicular to the wind direction.

If it is very windy, you may have to dig out a shallow depression or pit and set your fire at the bottom. To supply a draft, make the slope on the windward side of the pit more gradual than the slope of the other sides. Build a pit fire only on mineral soil and fill it in when you are through.

All three of these fireplaces are simple and take only minutes to construct. They make it easier for you to start and maintain your fires because they give you some control over the amount of draft reaching the fire. More importantly, they enclose the fire and make it safer.

Starting your fire. Now you are ready to lay your fire. If the fire-building surface is damp, it helps to put down a floor of sticks or logs and then build the fire on top of it. Arrange some tinder under a few pieces of wood that are no thicker than a piece of straw. Prop more twigs against these, gradually increasing the size of the twigs up to about finger thickness. You can arrange the twigs in a wigwam shape or lean them against the side of a log.

Light the tinder close to the ground. Fire burns up and away from the direction of the wind, so it helps if you have your back to the wind when you're lighting the fire. Give the fire plenty of air. It helps to blow on the fire from under it, on a level slightly above the ground. Feed the fire from the top on the side opposite the wind. Feed it gradually, first with the smaller pieces of wood, and then with the larger ones. Allow the fire to stabilize after each addition of several pieces of wood.

The best fires for cooking and keeping yourself warm are small, concentrated, and hot, and the best part of the fire to cook on is the coals. Keep the fire small and wait for a nice bed of coals to build up. You can help this process by crisscrossing the wood as you add it to the fire. Once the fire is burning well, it is easy to keep it going—Indian style. Put the ends of a few long sticks or logs in the fire, and as they burn, push them farther into it. They will give small flames and hot coals for hours. Notice that you don't have to spend time and energy cutting more wood, and when you're ready to sleep, simply pull the logs out of the fire.

As soon as the fire is stabilized, hang a pot of water over it to save cooking time, but wait for a bed of coals to build up before you put food on to bake, fry, or broil. The easiest way to suspend a pot over the fire is to make a simple crane: Jam the end of a forked stick into the ground a few inches from the fire and lay another stick through the fork, making an upside-down "V." Weigh down the ground-end of this stick with rocks and hang the pot from the angle where the sticks meet.

Putting your fire out. Before you leave the fire, put it out. Sprinkle a lot of water on the coals; stir them thoroughly with a stick, turning all the logs; then sprinkle copiously and stir again. Repeat this process until you can't feel any heat coming from the ashes. It is also very important to thoroughly wet the ground around the fire. Campfires that have not been properly drenched can not only reignite above the ground, but also creep underground, smolder, and resurface hours or even days after you're gone. A good rule to follow is that out means that you're able to stir the ashes with your hands.

CAMP CLEANLINESS

Dishes

Wash your dishes immediately after every meal so that you don't attract animals and insects to the campsite. If your meal included fats or animal products, you will need hot water to get the dishes clean, so hang a pot of water over the fire while you're drinking your tea or coffee. If you had only boiled grains, soup, and vegetables, this won't be necessary. Don't throw any scraps of food from the pans on the ground around the campsite. Either clean them off a good distance from the area or, better yet, scrape them into a stream. Use biodegradable soap. Sand makes an excellent pot scraper. So do horsetails because they contain so much silica. You may want to carry a lightweight copper scrubber; I cut one in two and take one half along with me. Rinse the dishes in the stream and pack them away.

Latrine

If you are camping in a designated campsite, use the latrine provided. If you are in the wilderness, go a good distance from the campsite to relieve yourself. Don't pick a spot near your water supply; go at least a couple of hundred feet away to a lower ground. Dig a shallow hole in the top soil, and when you're through, refill it. If you use toilet paper, take it back to the campfire and burn it. I prefer to use leaves or moss.

Covering Your Tracks

Before you leave your campsite, remove all signs of your visit. If you are unwilling to take the time to do this, don't go backpacking. There is not enough public land or wilderness area left where you can get away from signs of civilization as it is. Almost everyone has had the bad experience of taking a long peaceful walk through the woods only to arrive at a beautiful site ruined by rusting beer cans and old plastic bags. This feeling is multiplied a hundred times if you have hiked for miles through a wilderness area and find your campsite pocked by four old campfires full of balled-up tinfoil.

First, make sure that you have not left any food scraps around the area. Be careful not to leave any animal fats or meat products in the area because these have a strong enough odor to attract many scavengers. Burn all paper products. Pick up small scraps of paper from the area and burn them, too. Don't throw anything in the campfire that doesn't burn—this includes tinfoil.

Don't bury metal or plastic items. Clean them off and take them with you. I take my zip-lock bags home and use them again. After you have burned the paper items and put out the fire, remove the signs of your campfire. Scatter the stones that you used for the fireplace and re-fill the depression with the sand or gravel you scraped away. Stack any extra firewood neatly.

If you are in a designated camping area, clean the fire receptacle of any unburned trash. Replace any firewood you've used, if possible. If the last campers left the site a mess, take the time to clean up after them. Enough people are backpacking these days that the most popular areas are in danger of becoming "garbage dumps."

5. Nature, Animals, and Wild Foods

A little research done ahead of time on the plant and animal life that you will find in the area where you're headed will make your trip much more enjoyable. Visit your local library or bookstore during the planning stages of your trip. A list of suggested references is offered at the end of this chapter. Interesting pamphlets and inexpensive books on local flora and fauna can usually be obtained at park headquarters or in bookstores in the town or city closest to national parks.

Better yet, it is often possible to take a course at your hometown museum, agricultural extension service, Sierra Club, or university extension in wild edible plants, tree identification, wildlife indigenous to your area, and other topics. These courses will give you practical experience and will teach you faster than books. It is my experience that it is much better, and far less discouraging, to proceed slowly, learning a few plants and a few trees first, and then, as your curiosity takes over, add to your list as you go. While hiking, it is sheer joy to be able to recognize fresh wintergreen leaves for nibbling or Juneberries for dessert.

Track of a raccoon's hindfoot. Photo by Leonard Lee Rue III.

STALKING AND OBSERVING
WILD ANIMALS

When stalking and observing, don't just look for large mammals and birds. It is certainly thrilling to see moose and great blue herons, but you will almost always be able to find amphibians, reptiles, and even insects that are also fascinating. Learning about their lives will make you feel more and more at home in the outdoors. Sit next to a

Bear tracks. Photo by Leonard Lee Rue III.

pond and watch the voracious dragonflies guarding their territories and the water striders dashing around to check out struggling insects trapped in the surface film. Or watch a lizard stare down, strike and gobble down three fourths of a cicada in one lightning-fast movement.

Animals leave definite signs of their daily existence behind them, such as droppings (or scats), tracks, and trails. Look for this evidence to learn where to find the animals and to learn more about their lives. A good place to look for tracks is in the soft mud near streams or ponds.

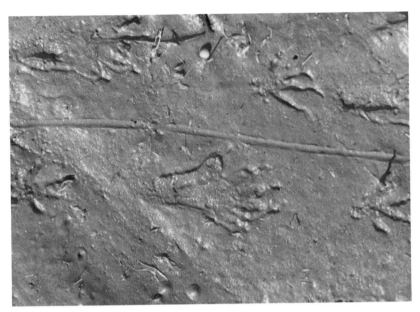

Muskrat tracks in soft mud. Note the tail drag. Photo by Leonard Lee Rue III.

Animals tend to visit the same territories every day or on some kind of a regular schedule and to travel on the same trails to come and go. Thus, if you wait and watch near these trails during the animals' times of activity, you will usually see several species. Little trails and ground tunnels through the grass are signs of mice and moles. Rabbits have larger runways leading to homes in dense vegetation near logs and fallen trees; muskrats make mud slides down the banks of creeks and streams into the water. Also look for animal homes and for favorite feeding spots. Hollow trees may house squirrels, raccoons, opossums, owls, or woodpeckers. Check the edge of the hole for bits of fur and look around the base of the tree for food remnants. Piles of empty pine seeds, acorns, and walnut shells show that a squirrel has been at work; a little elliptical ball of fur with mouse bones and teeth rolled up in it was regurgitated by an owl after a meal. Favorite spots for watching all wildlife include the edges of clearings or openings in the forest or woods, the shores of ponds, and the banks of streams and rivers.

Be sure you know when to look for certain animals and birds.

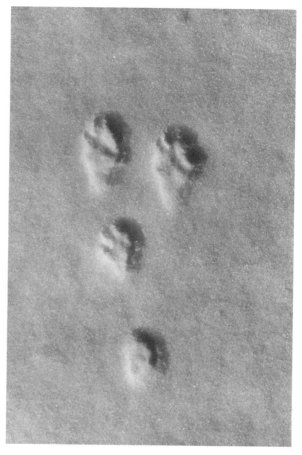

Tracks of a galloping red fox. Photo by Leonard Lee Rue III.

Chipmunks, gray and red squirrels, woodchucks, butterflies, and most birds are out during the day. Hoofed animals—moose, deer, antelope, and others—are active both day and night. Many rodents and carnivores are nocturnal; examples are flying squirrels and owls. The best time of day to see almost all birds and mammals actively foraging and moving about is early in the morning, during the hour or so preceding and after sunrise, and again fairly late in the evening, during the hour or so preceding and after sundown. After you've set up camp, sit down near the stream or pond where you found a lot of animal tracks and spend the dusk hours watching your neighbors. This is the time to see beaver, muskrats, swallows, and bats hard at work.

Remember, animals have very acute senses of hearing, smell, and sight, although the same animal does not necessarily have all three senses in a highly developed state. Therefore, you'll have the best luck if you just sit still. When you actively stalk animals, silence is essential. Be careful where and how you walk. Try to avoid dry sticks and leaves where possible. Adequate cover is helpful; so are clothes that blend into the landscape. Use simple camouflage such as leaves in your hat whenever possible. When you move, move slowly and cautiously, like the animals you're watching.

By adopting their habits you can not only find animals but also approach them closely enough to observe them fully. When moving while you are stalking, be sure to stop often and observe your surroundings. The motion of any large object (you, for example) is very visible in the woods and even more so in open areas. When you are still, however, you become a part of the surroundings and are much less visible. Other movements (the deer's, for example) then become obvious. If you want to watch deer, the best vantage point is from up in a tree, because deer rarely look up. They are very wary, however, of anything behind them.

There are a few other simple habits that are helpful in stalking and watching animals. First, look for and follow animals by moving upwind, not downwind. That is, walk into the wind or try to have it blow across your face from either side. If the wind's at your back, animals will smell you coming and will be long gone before you're able to see them. Second, try to keep the sun behind you and stay in the shade of your cover. Although this is not always possible, it is helpful because it makes you less visible to the animal, which has to look into the sun to look for you. If you are hiding behind an object, look around it to the side of it near the ground, and not over it. For example, if you're watching a moose from behind a bush or rock, look at him from either side near ground level, and not from over the top of the bush or rock. The same applies to hiding behind trees: Look from the side, low to the ground. Remember, the worst possible background you can have when trying to observe something without its observing you is the sky. Your silhouette against the sky is a dead giveaway. Good luck, and don't be discouraged; this takes practice, but it's well worth the effort. Your enjoyment of the woods will grow with each new bit of knowledge.

FORAGING FOR WILD FOODS

I have to begin this section with a word of caution: Before you begin sampling and eating any wild foods, be *sure* you know what you are eating. There are plants and berries that contain very potent poisons and are dangerous or even deadly. Pictures, drawings, and descriptions are very helpful in the process of identification, but the best way and the only way I recommend is to find someone who knows edible and poisonous plants and can point them out to you. In this way you can be sure.

When you identify a plant, carefully note the plant's habitat, as well as its leaf, flower, and bark characteristics. Soon you will know which plants to look for to get a free meal whether you are in a hardwood forest, an open field, or a swamp.

Since volumes have now been written on this subject, I'll simply include a few plants that are common and that I've eaten and enjoyed. I'll also recommend a few ways of preparing them.

Probably the two best-known groups of wild foods are the nuts and berries. Both nuts and berries formed integral parts of the diets of most Indian tribes of North America, and most are nourishing and delicious.

My Favorite Nut Trees

Oak. Many species of oak are found in North America, and all acorns are edible. However, the sweetest and most edible are from the white oaks—the oaks with the smooth-lobed leaves. I particularly like the large acorns (up to an inch long) of the chestnut oak. This tree has very deep vertical fissures in its bark; its leaves look like chestnut leaves

White oak acorns and leaf. Photo by Leonard Lee Rue III.

but with wavy margins. Roast white acorns over the fire and eat them like chestnuts. Black oaks, which have leaf margins that come to points, have acorns that are very bitter but may be eaten after boiling and roasting if you are really hungry!

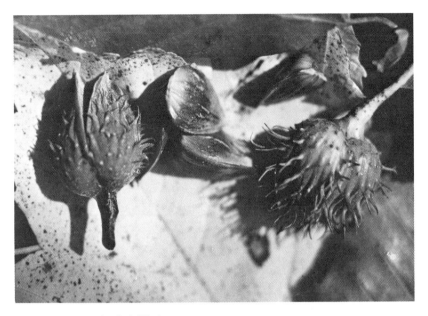

Beechnuts. Photo by Bob Wesley.

Beech. The silvery-gray, smooth bark, and the sometimes macabre contortions of the larger beeches, make this tree unmistakable. If you can find these small, triangular nuts (they seem to be among the first choices of squirrels), they are sweet and rich. Eat them raw.

Black walnut. The black walnut is a beautiful tree with black bark and compound, feathery, light-green leaves. The nut is enclosed in a tough, green husk, which turns brown when it has been on the ground for a time. The juice from the husk, which is a striking dark brown and was used as a dye by the Indians, will rapidly turn your hands a similar color. The nut, after aging, can be eaten raw; if unaged, it should be roasted or boiled. The flavor is probably familiar to you from ice cream and breads.

Butternut flowers. Photo by Bob Wesley.

Butternut (or white walnut). Butternut leaves are similar to black walnut leaves but are covered with sticky hairs. The nut is oblong, and the casing is green and very sticky. After it falls to the ground, it also turns brown, but does not contain the dyeing properties of the black walnut. This nut is one of my favorites; it's hard to extract the meat, but well worth the effort because it is very rich and oily when aged. Again, roast or boil the nuts if they are fresh.

Hickory. Hickories are found not only in the eastern United States but also as far west as the central Midwest. The shagbark is the easiest to identify because of the loose strips of bark hanging from the trunks of the older trees. This nut is also delicious raw. The husk resembles the walnut but is different in that it splits into four regular divisions when it ripens. This also seems to be among the first choices of the squirrels, so be early!

Pine. There are many different varieties of pine trees in the United States. The ones with the best tasting "pine nuts" grow primarily in the western United States. They formed an integral part of the diet of many western Indian tribes and are good either raw or roasted. If you are not sure which ones to eat, try them all because none are known to be poisonous. Suggested varieties: sugar pine, piñon pine, limber pine, and Coulter pine.

Fruits and Flowers

Blueberries. Wild blueberries are smaller than the cultivated varieties. They are found in acid soil, on low bushes, usually near swampy areas (lake shores, etc.). They are particularly abundant in northern areas such as Maine and Alaska. They're a favorite of bears, too, so keep an eye out while you're picking. If you can restrain yourself from putting them all in your mouth immediately, they are a great addition to pancakes, cereals, and other dishes.

Red raspberries, black raspberries, and blackberries. Each of these berries is easily recognizable. All are found on thorny, brambly, low-to medium-height bushes, in clearings or along the edges of forests, roads, trails, and fence lines. Look for them near old abandoned farms, if any are known to be in the area.

Wild strawberries. These appear in the early summer in sunny fields and clearings in the woods. The plants resemble cultivated strawberries, but the berries are smaller and much sweeter.

Low-bush blueberries. Photo by Bob Wesley.

Black raspberries (black caps). Photo by Bob Wesley.

Blackberries. Photo by Bob Wesley.

Wild strawberries. Photo by Bob Wesley.

Serviceberries, sometimes called Juneberries. Photo by Bob Wesley.

Serviceberries or Juneberries. These relatively small trees are among the first trees to blossom in the spring, and they have beautiful, sweet-smelling white flowers. As a rule, you can find them at the edge of the woods. The berries look very much like "blueberries on trees," are blue to bluish-red when ripe, and are delicious raw. Also, use them as you would use blueberries. They are a favorite of the birds so, again, be early!

Mulberries. Mulberry trees can be recognized by their leaf shapes. The same tree bears both heart-shaped and lobed leaves. The berries

Elderberry flowers. Photo by Bob Wesley.

resemble blackberries because they are composed of many small sections; they're a treat, raw or cooked.

Elderberries. These miniature berries are found in clusters on bushes. The flower resembles "Queen Anne's lace." The berries are reddish to dark purple when ripe and may be eaten raw. However, these berries have a peculiar taste and are best when added to some cooked food, such as cereals or bread. They are rich in vitamin C.

Much tastier than the elderberries themselves are the flower clusters. They have a long blooming season, and you may find them during much of the summer. Add them to pancake batter or quick breads and muffins for a delightful flavor.

Black locust flowers. Photo by Bob Wesley.

Black locust blossoms. Black locust trees have very dark bark and compound leaves with egg-shaped leaflets. A pair of short spines are found at the base of each leaf stalk. In the late spring, after most other trees have finished blooming, the black locust produces clusters of white blossoms that look like pea flowers. These are even better than elderberry blossoms. Eat them raw or dip them in batter and fry them.

Wild grapes. Photo by Bob Wesley.

Other Fruits

Wild grapes. These are easily recognizable by their vines and their typical grape leaves. They are usually found climbing near the edges of fields, woods, fence lines, and clearings. Both grapes and leaves are edible. Boil the leaves for a few minutes and stuff with grains.

Rose hips. Photo by Bob Wesley.

Rose hips. These are the fruit of the wild rose and should be picked after the first frost, when they become much sweeter. Delicious raw or cooked, they contain copious amounts of vitamin C, but unfortunately are mostly seeds.

Nodding wild onion. Photo by Bob Wesley.

Wild Salads and Vegetables

Wild onions and wild garlic. The stems look and smell very much liked the stems of any young cultivated onion and can be found growing almost anywhere there is sufficient water. The entire plant can be eaten either raw or cooked. If you make any kind of pan bread or bannock, this makes an excellent flavoring. Wild leeks are especially good. They have broader stems (leaves) than the others and can be found in

Dandelion. Photo by Bob Wesley.

wet forests in late spring. If you are lucky enough to get some, make onion soup by sautéing the leeks (in a little fat) and adding them to bouillon. Cream of leek or onion soup can be made by adding powdered milk.

Burdock. This plant is easily distinguishable by its burrs, which you do not want to get into your hair. In the spring the young stalks, cooked or raw, make a good green for a salad. I've also eaten the roots mashed and cooked in bread and scrambled eggs and in wild fish and vegetable stew.

Dandelions. In the spring, the young, tender leaves are excellent raw in a salad. The roots may be eaten but tend to be bitter and are much better when cooked. Other good greens to gather for salads or to eat cooked like spinach include sorrel, lamb's quarters, purslane, and mustard. Mix them if you can't find enough of one kind.

Sorrel. Photo by Bob Wesley.

Lamb's quarters. Photo by Bob Wesley.

Cattails. These are found only in marshes or other wet areas. The light-colored parts of the new shoots in the spring and the new spike, or cattail, of this plant are excellent when roasted or fried with herbs. The roots are also edible but very starchy; a paste may be made of them and added to bread or used to thicken stew or soup. The roots can be baked and eaten. Indians made bread from cattail starch.

Broad-leaved cattail. Photo by Bob Wesley.

Arrowheads. Small plants, sometimes called "arrowhead pond weed," their large leaves resemble arrowheads. They are also found near or in the water. Only the bulbs at the end of the threadlike roots are eaten, but when roasted these taste like exceptionally good new potatoes. This was another favorite of the Indians.

Fiddleheads. Photo by Bob Wesley.

Fiddleheads. Actually this is the name for the young, curled-up heads of forest ferns. These tender, sweet fronds may be gathered in the spring, and although not as nutritious as some of the other wild plants, they are delicious either raw or cooked.

Solomon's seal. This is another spring plant, which grows on forest floors. You can eat the tender, young shoots raw or cooked. The roots, when cooked (baked in or roasted over the campfire), taste very much like parsnips or rutabagas.

Morel mushrooms. Photo by Bob Wesley.

Mushrooms. Do not eat mushrooms unless you are shown the edible varieties by someone who knows what he is doing. There are only two varieties that a beginner should think about trying: morels and puffballs.

Morels are the easiest mushrooms to recognize and also among the tastiest. They are shaped like pine cones and grow in the late spring. All varieties are edible. Sauté them lightly over your campfire. They are a real luxury on a backpacking trip.

Giant puffball. Photo by Bob Wesley.

Puffballs should be eaten only in the early stages, when their insides are moist and cheesy. Sliced and fried, they are delicious. Like the morel, they are a welcome addition to any meal. Before eating, cut through the puffball and make sure that it is not the early, or button, stage of another type of mushroom, which could be poisonous. That is, make sure the inside is full and of a uniform texture.

Again, I don't recommend sampling any mushrooms until someone points the edible ones out to you.

Wintergreen. Photo by Bob Wesley.

Beverages

Mints. Leaves and stems from any of the mints make refreshing teas. You can recognize plants in this family by their square stems and two-lipped flowers. Crush a leaf to smell the minty fragrance. My favorite is peppermint, which has a red stem and dark green leaves and grows in moist areas.

Spearmint. Photo by Bob Wesley.

Fresh wintergreen leaves may be nibbled raw or steeped to make another good tea. Wintergreen is a low-growing plant on the forest floor and has dark green leaves. It has red berries that also taste of winter-green and are a good treat while you're walking.

Sassafras. Photo by Bob Wesley.

Basswood or linden. These trees have large heart-shaped leaves and flower in early summer. The tiny flowers have an incredibly rich honey smell. Pick some flowers and throw them into boiling water for a sweet, fragrant tea.

Sassafras. Sassafras is a shrub or small tree that may be recognized by its varied leaves, some mitten-shaped, others with three lobes. The roots may be used for a rootbeer-flavored tea. After cutting them into fine shavings, boil them for twenty minutes. This aromatic brew was used as a spring tonic and blood thinner by the Indians of the eastern United States.

A WORD ABOUT WEATHER

A little knowledge about predicting weather is sure to come in handy when you're on a backpacking trip. The best means of forecasting the weather without the use of thermometers, barometers, and radio stations will come through observing winds and clouds.

Winds

The winds in North America generally come from the west bringing the weather with them. Westerly winds, during the summer, usually mean clear, cool weather. However, on the Pacific coast and in western Florida, westerly winds come in off the ocean bringing a lot of moisture. The north wind, coming from polar regions, also brings cooler or cold weather. If the wind is from directly north or northwest it probably means clear, cool weather. Winds from the south are coming from tropical regions and are generally warm. The wind from the southwest is the hottest of all during the summer months. Wind from the southeast brings rain. East of the Rockies, winds along a warm front usually blow from the east or northeast and forecast rain.

Clouds

The clouds are carried by the winds. The three main types of clouds are easy to recognize. Cirrus clouds are made up of tiny ice crystals and always look white and feathery or tufted. These are the highest clouds in the sky, anywhere from six to nine miles up. Cumulus clouds are the big, puffy, heaped-up clouds. The bottom of cumulus clouds may be only a few hundred feet above the ground, while the tops reach up over a mile. Stratus clouds come in layered sheets and cover large areas. These are the lowest clouds, from about 400 to 2,000 feet above the earth. Any cloud from which rain or snow is falling is called a nimbus cloud. Alto- is joined to the beginning of the name of any type of cloud to designate that the cloud is particularly high above the ground. The various cloud names are used in combination with each other to describe intermediate forms, since clouds are often changing from one type to another.

The huge, puffy white clouds that are fun to watch because of their fantastic shapes are cumulus clouds. If they start to pile up on hot summer days into gigantic towering forms with flat bottoms, they are changing to thunderheads. This means that a thunderstorm or a heavy rainstorm is about to start. Altocumulus clouds are typical summer clouds that indicate fair weather. They are medium-sized, cumulus-type clouds that float across the sky at great heights. When these clouds break up into series of tiny puffs, they have changed to cirrocumulus clouds and may presage unsettled weather with showers.

When a storm is on the way, a series of different types of clouds helps to let you know how soon to expect precipitation. First, wispy, windblown cirrus clouds appear high in the sky forecasting rain within two days. Next, these fade into one another, forming a thin layer of cirrostratus. When the moon shines through these clouds at night, you see them as a ring around the moon. Cirrostratus clouds darken and drop closer to earth as they change to altostratus clouds. When they turn to a solid, low-lying blanket, completely blocking the sun, they are pure stratus clouds, and rain is due in six or seven hours. The rain arrives in black nimbostratus clouds.

Now that you know some general rules for forecasting weather that work most of the time, it's fun to look for other little signals. Rain is probably on its way when the sunset is dark and dull and the sunrise is red. Bad weather is also coming when smoke from your campfire remains close to the ground, when bats and swallows chase insects close to the pond surface, and when there is no or very little dew on your tent in the morning. On the other hand, expect fair weather when there is a beautiful red sunset or when the sun goes down as a huge flaming-orange ball. Other hopeful signs are bats and swallows flying high, campfire smoke rising straight up into the air, and heavy dew and misty valleys in the mornings.

SELECTED READINGS

The widest selection of field guides is found in the Peterson Field Guide Series (Houghton Mifflin Co.). All of them are excellent. The ones you may be particularly interested in include:

Murie, Olaus J.: A Field Guide to Animal Tracks
Burt, William H., and Grossenheider, Richard P.: A Field Guide to the Mammals
Peterson, Roger Tory: A Field Guide to the Birds
Petrides, George A.: A Field Guide to Trees and Shrubs
Menzel, Donald H.: A Field Guide to the Stars and Planets
Peterson, Roger Tory, and McKenny, Margaret: A Field Guide to Wildflowers of Northeastern and North-Central North America
Craighead, John J., Craighead, Frank C., and Davis, Ray J.: A Field Guide to Rocky Mountain Wildflowers
Niehaus, Theodore F.: A Field Guide to Pacific States Wildflowers
Borror, Donald J., and White, Richard E.: A Field Guide to the Insects of America North of Mexico

The Golden Press Nature Guides (Western Publishing Co., Inc.) are also good. They include:

Brockman, C. Frank: Trees of North America (edited by Herbert S. Zim and George S. Fichter)
Robbins, Chandler, et al.: Birds of North America: A Guide to Field Identification

Other recommended books include:

Smith, Alexander H., and Weber, Nancy: The Mushroom Hunter's Field Guide (The University of Michigan Press)
Books by Euell Gibbons, especially Stalking the Wild Asparagus (David McKay Co., Inc.)

6. On Being Lost and Surviving It

A SURVIVAL PRIMER

Once again, I want to stress that *before* you go into a wilderness area, you should notify the park authorities and/or friends as to your expected destination and length of stay. Then, if you do get lost, you will have nothing to worry about. Aerial and ranger reconnaissance is so good these days that chances are you will be found much sooner than you think. The only thing you will have to worry about if you are alone in the wilderness for a length of time is your own fear. Fear makes you unable to think and plan carefully and increases your chances of doing some damage to yourself by acting hastily. Fear of the unknown is easy to dispel with reason and knowledge. The more you know about the area you have entered, the better off you will be. Becoming familiar with the local climate, topography, and plant and animal life will help you to conquer any imaginary fears.

Assuming you've become lost, the number-one thing to do is nothing—yes nothing—until you take your pack off, sit down, take a deep breath, and think about what's happening and what's happened. *Don't be in a hurry*, continue to think and act slowly and deliberately, and *don't panic*. The wilderness was man's first home. If you have a map, compass, or watch, orient yourself to the basic directions. If you don't have one of these items use the sun's position to find out approximately where you are, where you've come from, and where you want to be. Mentally retrace your steps and try to think where you last left the trail, where the sun was in relation to the direction you were hiking, or where and when you were last sure of your position. If you can remember any of this information, slowly and calmly act on it, returning to where you were last sure of your surroundings. Mountains, rivers, streams, trails, and other landmarks are there just waiting to help you out.

If you're really hopelessly lost in a large, impenetrable wilderness area, the best thing you can do is *stay put*, and build a larger-than-normal, smoky fire. Build the fire and then almost smother it with wet leaves or other damp vegetation. Of course, take the necessary precautions, such as clearing the space, so that you don't set the forest on fire. However, if after several days no one finds you and you did not leave word with someone as to where you were going or when you would be back, determine as best as you can the best course to follow using the instruments and knowledge you have. Travel slowly and very deliberately toward a destination, observing and checking your course of travel frequently. If there is a stream or river in the area, follow it *downstream*. It will eventually lead to a larger river or to a sedentary body of water, such as a lake or ocean, which may be identifiable, and is more than likely inhabited.

During the time that you are alone in the wilderness you will have three basic needs: water, food, and shelter. Of these, water is the most important, so find a good source of water as soon as possible. If you stay where you are and don't exert yourself very much you will not even need much water. If you don't have any source of water, don't eat because your body uses up water when digesting and eliminating waste products. If you have a limited supply of food and water with you, don't eat or drink for the first 24 hours. After this time, ration your supplies and your body will use the food more efficiently. Don't worry about your food supply. You can fast for weeks and still stay in excellent physical condition. Keeping yourself protected as much as possible from extremes in temperature will lower your body's need for food and water.

Actually, the possibility of getting lost while backpacking in an area where water and/or food are not available is remote. All you really have to do is locate and use the natural resources at hand.

Finding Water When You're Lost

Finding water is relatively easy once you know where to look. One important point to remember is that the water table – the surface below which the rocks of the earth's crust are saturated with water – is probably not far from the surface in any low, green, heavily forested or vegetated area. Therefore it is much easier to locate water in lower areas – meadows, valleys, or river valleys – than it is on the plateaus, in the foothills, or on the mountainsides. Water is so close to the surface in a river's flood plain or any area where cattails grow that it can usually be obtained by digging a small hole. If this doesn't work, try carefully following a few large game trails; these should eventually lead to a water source.

Finding Food When You're Lost

In a pinch, you can eat almost anything if you're hungry enough:

It was thought if their [Narrangansett, Nipmuck, and Wampanoag Indians] corn were cut down, they would starve and dy with hunger: and all their corn that could be found, was destroyed, and they driven from that little they had in store, into the woods in the midst of winter... strangely did the Lord provide for them, that I did not see (all the time I was among them) one man, woman, or child, dy with hunger.

Though many times they would eat that, that a Hog or a Dog would hardly touch.... The chief and commonest food was ground nuts: They also eat nuts and acorns, Harty-choaks, Lilly roots, Ground Beans, and several other weeds and roots, that I know not.

They would pick up old bones, and cut them to pieces at the joynts, and if they were full of wormes and magots, they would scald them over the fire to make the vermin come out, and then boile them, and drink up the liquor, and then beat the great ends of them in a mortar, and so eat them. They would eat horses gut and ears, and all sorts of wild birds which they would catch: also, Bear, Vennison, Beaver, Tortoise, Frogs, Squirrels, Dogs, Skunks, Rattlesnakes; yea, the very bark of trees. (*The Portable North American Indian Reader*, edited by Frederick Turner III, "The Captivity of Mary Rowlandson," pp. 351–352)

You don't have to trap a rabbit to supply yourself with food. Start off with the simplest life forms that are found in great abundance and don't take special skill to collect.

A little knowledge about wild plants of the area (see preceding chapter) is very useful, but if you don't see any plants that are familiar, there are some general rules you can follow: All grass seeds are edible. Fiddleheads and the roots of many ferns are edible, and none is known to be poisonous, so you can safely try them. The white inner bark of many trees, especially birches, willows, and poplars, is edible either raw or cooked. In cold climates, where no plant food can be seen, try digging for tubers or roots where you see dried plant stalks. Many aquatic plants also have tubers that are available throughout the year.

Insects can be found almost anywhere and are easy to catch. Grasshoppers can be eaten. They are more palatable cooked, but first pull off the head and the glands attached to it, as these glands may contain offensive chemicals. Dragonflies and cicadas are also edible. Dig through rotting logs to find beetle grubs. Don't eat caterpillars, because many have offensive chemicals in glands or in their hairs.

Streams and ponds are especially rich in animal food. Crayfish are abundant in streams; look for them under rocks. Cook them before you eat them. Frogs and salamanders should be skinned and gutted before eating them. Mollusks, such as aquatic snails, should only be eaten cooked; they may contain harmful parasites. Snakes and turtles are also edible, and some are delicious, but be careful of poisonous snakes and snapping turtles. Of course, you can try to catch fish if you have emergency fishing equipment along. All birds and mammals are edible, but most are hard to catch. However, if you watch them during feeding times, they may lead you to a food source that you can use, too.

Finding Shelter When You're Lost

Assuming that you do not have your tent with you, first look for natural shelters, such as a large fallen evergreen tree, a large log over which you can easily construct a shelter of two poles and some leaves, a cave, or a natural depression. The idea is to try to get out of the wind and cold and stay relatively dry. Check your shelter for insects and animals in daylight before you go to sleep.

7 Common Problems

I have included this section because there are several hassles that are so common that almost every backpacker has encountered them on one trip or another. Your chances of having any serious problems on a backpacking trip, such as accidents or getting lost, are very slim. However, you will almost certainly encounter a couple of the following situations during the first few times you go out. If you are prepared as much as possible in advance, these will be minor irritations. But, if you are unprepared, some of these problems could ruin your whole trip.

THE FIRST TWO DAYS

The first couple of days of your trip you may feel tired or even exhausted. Of course, this will depend on the amount of time you are used to spending outdoors, the hiking pace you set, the terrain, and your physical condition when you start. You may also be slightly stiff and sore from hiking and carrying a pack. There are two ways to lessen this problem. First, make absolutely sure before you set out that your pack weighs as little as possible. Don't take anything that is not essential, especially on your first trip. Second, keep going, proceeding at your own rate. Usually by the third day all your small aches and pains will disappear and you will suddenly begin to feel exhilarated and full of energy. You will relax, your senses will become more acute, your body will feel more vigorous and healthy. This period of physical adjustment to strenuous exercise and to living in the outdoors takes a few days (unless you're used to it) and is completely normal.

You may also have a vague feeling of uneasiness at the beginning. Rugged, wild scenery, silence broken only by unaccustomed noises, and trails covered with animal instead of human tracks are all beautiful and exciting but may also be a little unnerving until you're used to them. Again, the more you know about the geography and animal life of the region you're entering, the more comfortable you will feel. In a few days you won't want to go back to civilization.

In many of the wilderness areas you will still see bear tracks, which may increase your uneasiness a little. Your chances of seeing a bear are fairly slim since they are rather shy, except in areas where they are regularly fed by campers! Consider yourself lucky if you do get a chance to watch a bear in the wild. If you do feel nervous about bears, just keep a few facts in mind. There are really only three situations in which wild bears are potentially dangerous. First, if you surprise them in dense thickets, for example, while you are berry picking (they love berries, too). Second, if you find yourself between a mother and her cubs. Third, if you leave your food in your tent. The first situation can be avoided by giving the bear fair warning of your approach – this is your responsibility as the intruder – by whistling (some people carry a whistle), singing, or making other loud human noises. The second situation can be avoided by staying away from apparently abandoned cubs – mother is not far off. The solution to the third is, obviously, don't put food in your tent. (See section on Setting up your camp.) If you do come face-to-face with a bear on a trail, don't move quickly. Back up very slowly and talk to it quietly if you can get your voice together. He will probably be retreating faster than you are!

FOOT TROUBLE

Blisters

Blisters are probably the most common backpacking problem of all. Even though your boots are well broken in, the extra weight and long distances are especially hard on your feet. If you are unprepared for blisters, they can become so disabling that you may have to cancel the trip, limp home, and sit out the rest of your vacation on the front porch. However, if you take adequate precautions against blisters and have supplies to treat any that appear, they are no more than a minor annoyance.

The best protections against blisters, besides boots that fit and are well broken in, are clean, dry socks. Again, take enough pairs so that you can wash some out on the trail and still start each day with fresh, dry socks. Hang your wet socks to dry on the outside of your pack while hiking. Wet, dirty socks abrade your feet. Heavy wool socks are best for hiking because they help prevent chafing by absorbing perspiration. It is also helpful to sprinkle talcum powder inside your socks, and also on the inside of your boot, especially in the heel area. Talc will help absorb moisture and let your foot slide more easily in the boot.

Blisters can form before you realize it, so pay attention to your feet. Foam-backed moleskin is both a preblister treatment and a blister remedy and works better than anything else I've tried. If you feel a blister forming, if your heel is beginning to get sensitive, or even if you think there's a possibility of getting a blister in a certain area of your foot, *stop immediately*. Tape a piece of moleskin over the sensitive area with surgical tape. Place the soft side of the moleskin against your skin and the surgical tape on the sticky back. This will prevent you from pulling your skin off when you remove the moleskin. Use surgical tape because it is very thin, doesn't lump up and thus cause a worse blister, and peels off easily without removing pieces of your skin. Remove the moleskin at night to let your skin harden. You can reuse the same piece of moleskin the next day, by cutting the tape off around the edges and securing it with fresh tape. If you do develop a blister filled with liquid, leave it alone, cover it with moleskin, and do the best you can. If your blister is already broken, clean it with soap and water. Put a little antibiotic ointment (Bacitracin) on it and cover it with a bandage. Keep it covered when you're wearing shoes until new skin closes the blister. Moleskin will keep blisters from hurting and allow them to heal quickly.

Ingrown Toenail

An ingrown toenail is a nail that is pushing into the skin. The toe usually becomes infected and causes a lot of pain. Ultimately ingrown toenails stem from cutting your nails improperly. However, they may begin to cause trouble while you are backpacking because of the additional pressure on your feet from carrying the weight of your pack. To prevent ingrown toenails, cut your big toenails straight across; never round them off at the corners. To attain temporary relief from an ingrown toenail, the skin flap may be taped away from the nail, the toe soaked in hot water, and a "V" cut in the central part of the toenail.

RAIN

Just had an early morning downpour, or it's been rainy and damp for three days, and everything is soaked? And you forgot to store some kindling and small stuff in the corner of your tent or in the bottom of your pack? Don't worry; you can still have a fire to dry out in front of and cook breakfast over. The trick here is to be able to find enough dry kindling and finger-sized wood to get the fire going, because once the fire is hot, you can feed it with wet wood.

If you can find a standing dead tree, take some of the finger-thick branches and shave off their exteriors with your knife—even continuous rain usually doesn't soak very far into this type of wood. Now make a pile of dry wood chips or shave these into fuzz sticks. Make five or six of these and use them, shavings down, for your kindling. Alternately, pick the biggest, oldest, thickest evergreen you can find. Even after days of hard rain, there are probably dry twigs way under it on the ground or on its trunk. You can also look for dry twigs on the underside of large leaning or fallen trees. Resinous pine knots on dead evergreens or resinous parts of old stumps also make good tinder when it's been raining because they contain so much sap. Birch bark (from dead birch trees) burns very well when wet.

If it's really raining hard, it may be more convenient to pull out your backpacking stove and set it up near the entrance to your tent. In severely inclement weather, however, it is comforting to know that uncooked food almost invariably contains more nourishment than cooked food.

If you're going to hike in the rain, make sure that any down articles you have are well protected. I carry two or three plastic garbage bags for this purpose. I put my sleeping bag in one, and it keeps perfectly dry even though the bag is strapped on my pack frame. If your sleeping bag or other down articles do get wet, do not dry them by the fire. The nylon melts very easily and the down will become compacted. Dry them, when you can, in the sun and air.

OTHER ANNOYANCES

Insects

For your first backpacking trips, avoid those times of the year when the bugs are at their worst. This means finding out in advance what months the mosquitoes, black flies, and no-see-'ums are at their most numerous in the area you are planning to visit. Particularly avoid the height of black-fly season because black-fly bites are especially irritating.

Once you're out on the trail, there's actually not too much you can do about insects except learn to live with them. Wear your lightweight, loose-fitting pants and long-sleeved shirt. Tuck your pant legs into your socks, and, if things get really bad, wear your mosquito head-net.

Make smoky campfires at your campsite and sit as close to them as possible. Let your smell get good and strong; don't use sweet-smelling soap or shampoo. A strong, smoky smell attracts fewer insects.

Camp Thieves

If you camp in an area that a lot of sloppy picnickers have visited before you, chances are that you may lose a good portion of your food, not to mention pieces of your pack, to marauding animals. I *always* avoid these campsites if at all possible; I once had four pockets of my pack chewed through within half an hour of my arrival. A few practices may discourage the little pickpockets. Be very careful when you're packing your food. Don't be sloppy. Make sure that all plastic bags and containers are free from holes, tightly sealed, and clean on the outside— after each use. Don't let granola crumbs collect in the corners of your pack and keep the pockets tightly zipped at all times. If you have a heavy rain poncho, wrap it around your pack. You can also try hanging your pack as you would to frustrate a bear. (See section on Setting up your camp.) Above all, keep your campsite clean!

Contact Poisons

Make sure you know how to recognize poison ivy, poison oak, and poison sumac. All three have compound leaves and berries that range in color from grayish-green to white. Poison ivy hs three shiny green leaflets with a few coarse teeth that turn reddish-brown in the fall when the plant also bears clusters of white berries. It usually looks like a small shrub but can climb to great heights if it has support. Poison oak also has three leaflets, but they resemble oak leaves, with wavy margins. Poison sumac grows only in wet, swampy areas. It looks like the other sumacs, but it is not hairy, its leaf stalks are not winged, and it has white fruit.

All parts of these plants are poisonous, and direct contact with them causes an itchy skin rash with little bumps that turn into blisters. You are particularly susceptible when you are overheated and sweating. You can also contract the rash by touching clothing that has brushed against the plants or, worse yet, by breathing or coming in contact with the smoke of a fire that contains poison ivy.

If you have been walking through an area with lots of poison ivy or oak growing around the trail, wash thoroughly with soap after you have reached your campsite. Wash your clothes before you wear them again.

If you know that you are particularly sensitive to these plants, take your normal medicine with you on your backpacking trip.

Poison sumac. Photo by Bob Wesley.

I hope you are able to enjoy some of the beauty and solitude of the world's wilderness areas. The simple wonders of Mother Earth are truly mysterious and refreshing. Observe, experience, and enjoy them but leave them as you found them—wild, natural, and unspoiled.

Index